PEARSON
REALITY CENTRAL
Readings in the Real World

PEARSON

Upper Saddle River, New Jersey • Boston, Massachusetts
Chandler, Arizona • Glenview, Illinois • Shoreview, Minnesota

ISBN 978-0-13-367436-1
ISBN 0-13-367436-3

8 9 10   VO11   14 13 12 11 10

TABLE OF CONTENTS

 Unit 1 BQ: What is the best way to find the truth?

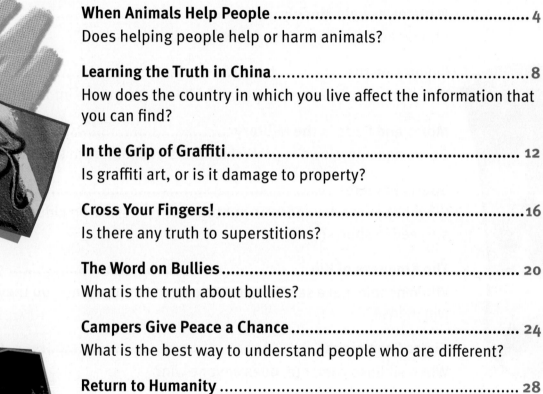

When Animals Help People 4
Does helping people help or harm animals?

Learning the Truth in China 8
How does the country in which you live affect the information that you can find?

In the Grip of Graffiti 12
Is graffiti art, or is it damage to property?

Cross Your Fingers! 16
Is there any truth to superstitions?

The Word on Bullies 20
What is the truth about bullies?

Campers Give Peace a Chance 24
What is the best way to understand people who are different?

Return to Humanity 28
How do events in our lives shape the truth of who we are?

Luol Deng: A True Winner 32
How has Deng's past made him the true winner he is today?

TABLE OF CONTENTS

 Unit 2 BQ: Does every conflict have a winner?

Athletes as Role Models 40
Should athletes be role models who help others "win"?

Coyotes on the Go 44
Does anyone win when people and wild animals come into conflict?

Moms and Dads in the Military 48
Do we need new laws to protect mothers and fathers in the military?

Sports Parents 52
What happens when parents put too much pressure on kids to succeed in sports?

The Kindness of Kin 56
When people make sacrifices to become kinship parents, do they win or lose?

Sister Champions 60
When siblings compete, does anyone win?

Two Views of the Zoo 64
Should animals be put in zoos?

Either Too Young or Too Old 68
Is there a "right age" to start voting or stop working?

 Unit 3 BQ: What should we learn?

Travel to Mars...76
What do we need to learn about Mars to live there?

Look Who's Talking 80
What can we learn from differences in speaking styles?

Making Sport of Tradition 84
Why is it important to learn about cultures different from your own?

In Your Dreams 88
What can we learn from our dreams?

The Titans Remember 92
How do people who are different learn to work together?

The Price of Discovery...96
Is the information we gain from space exploration worth the cost?

Someone Has to Do It 100
What can we learn from people who do dangerous jobs?

Have No Fear 104
How can people learn to overcome phobias?

TABLE OF CONTENTS

 Unit 4 BQ: What is the best way to communicate?

Thinking of You..112
Are greeting cards a good way to communicate feelings?

Word on the Wire..116
Do cell phones belong in school?

A Show of Strength..120
How do real-life heroes show courage?

The Big Money..124
What message do we send with the salaries we pay to "stars"?

Pay Days...128
What do families communicate by paying kids an allowance?

The Music Mix..132
When music takes different forms, does it send different messages?

Follow Your Star..136
What does people's fascination with celebrity life communicate?

The Age Factor..140
What message about aging do older athletes communicate?

Unit 5 BQ: Do others see us more clearly than we see ourselves?

How Attitude Helps.. 148
Do negative thoughts keep you down?

Happiness: A Two-Way Street? 152
What does it take to be happy?

Called Out 156
Why might an intervention be the best way to help someone?

Pushing Buttons...160
What is the best way to handle hurtful gossip?

TABLE OF CONTENTS

 Unit 6 BQ: Community or individual—which is more important?

The Great Dress Debate 168
Is individuality more important than following the rules?

Commanding the Weather 172
Should we try to control the weather or let nature take its course?

Restoring Cities from the Ground Up 176
Can an urban garden really help turn a community around?

What It Takes to Lead 180
What makes a good leader?

Rebuilding Communities 184
What does it take to make a community unite and rebuild?

The Irresistible Urban Myth 188
What purposes do urban myths serve?

The Ripple Effect 192
Do small, individual efforts really matter, or must large, group efforts be made for real change to occur?

Trickster Appeal Revealed! 196
What makes trickster characters so appealing?

ABOUT YOUR BOOK

The What and Why of this Book

This book is a collection of articles written with you in mind. The articles are on real-life topics you and your friends might talk about. In fact, you may even disagree about them. This is because the topics often have two or more sides.

The Big Question

The articles in this book are broken down into units. Each unit has a Big Question like this one: **How do we decide what is true?** After you read the articles in a unit, you will use them to answer the Unit Big Question. Each article also has its own main question for you to think about as you read. This question connects the article to the Unit BQ.

Unit Opener

Each unit begins with an opener that shows a real-life situation and connects to the Unit BQ. Use the opener to prepare for the unit articles.

The Big Question
Here is the Unit Big Question.

Introduction
This paragraph connects you to the situation shown in the art.

Prompt
Use this question to put yourself into the situation pictured.

Kick It Off

Before each article you will find a Kick It Off page. This page will help you get ready to read the article.

Real-Life Connection
Use this section to think about the article topic. Here you may also see a graphic organizer to help you collect ideas.

Word Bank
Here are words that are important in the article. Notice that they are bold.

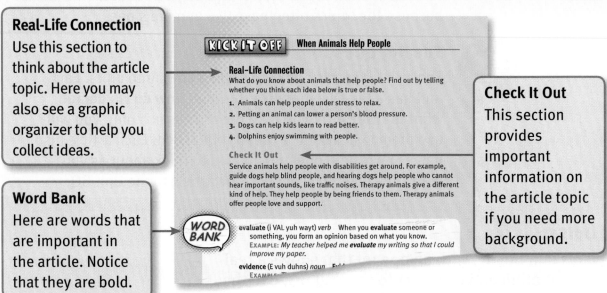

KICK IT OFF When Animals Help People

Real-Life Connection
What do you know about animals that help people? Find out by telling whether you think each idea below is true or false.

1. Animals can help people under stress to relax.
2. Petting an animal can lower a person's blood pressure.
3. Dogs can help kids learn to read better.
4. Dolphins enjoy swimming with people.

Check It Out
Service animals help people with disabilities get around. For example, guide dogs help blind people, and hearing dogs help people who cannot hear important sounds, like traffic noises. Therapy animals give a different kind of help. They help people by being friends to them. Therapy animals offer people love and support.

WORD BANK
evaluate (i VAL yuh wayt) *verb*   When you **evaluate** someone or something, you form an opinion based on what you know.
EXAMPLE: *My teacher helped me evaluate my writing so that I could improve my paper.*

evidence (E vuh duhns) *noun*   Evid...
EXAMPLE: Th...

Check It Out
This section provides important information on the article topic if you need more background.

The Article

These short articles are like the ones you might read in magazines or on-line. Before you read, look for these features to get you started:

Unit Big Question
The Unit Big Question is repeated here to help you remember.

Article
Now the article begins. Do not forget to read the title!

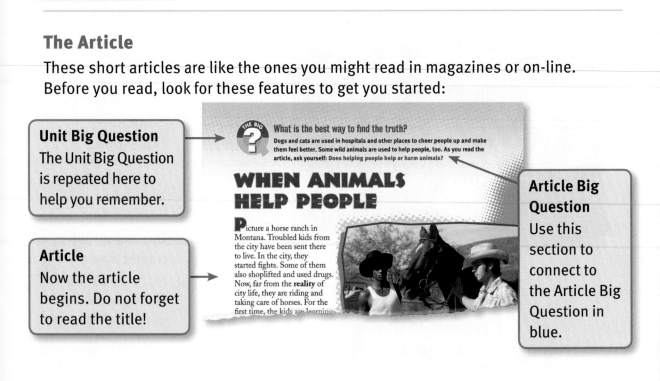

THE BIG ? What is the best way to find the truth?
Dogs and cats are used in hospitals and other places to cheer people up and make them feel better. Some wild animals are used to help people, too. As you read the article, ask yourself: **Does helping people help or harm animals?**

WHEN ANIMALS HELP PEOPLE

Picture a horse ranch in Montana. Troubled kids from the city have been sent there to live. In the city, they started fights. Some of them also shoplifted and used drugs. Now, far from the **reality** of city life, they are riding and taking care of horses. For the first time, the kids are learning

Article Big Question
Use this section to connect to the Article Big Question in blue.

Read the Article

As you read the article you will notice several tools. These tools are here to help explain the article and to keep information organized and clear.

Vocabulary
Word banks terms and their forms are set bold to help you collect ideas.

Subheads
Subheads help you preview what this section of the article will be about.

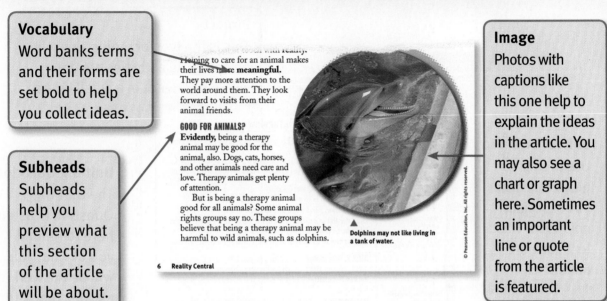

GOOD FOR ANIMALS?
Evidently, being a therapy animal may be good for the animal, also. Dogs, cats, horses, and other animals need care and love. Therapy animals get plenty of attention.

But is being a therapy animal good for all animals? Some animal rights groups say no. These groups believe that being a therapy animal may be harmful to wild animals, such as dolphins.

Helping to care for an animal makes their lives more **meaningful.** They pay more attention to the world around them. They look forward to visits from their animal friends.

▲ Dolphins may not like living in a tank of water.

6 Reality Central

Image
Photos with captions like this one help to explain the ideas in the article. You may also see a chart or graph here. Sometimes an important line or quote from the article is featured.

Wrap It Up

After each article you will find a Wrap It Up box. This section is here to help you check your understanding and summarize what you have learned.

Find It on the Page
The answers to these questions can be found in the article.

Use Clues
You will have to use clues from the article and your own thinking to answer these questions.

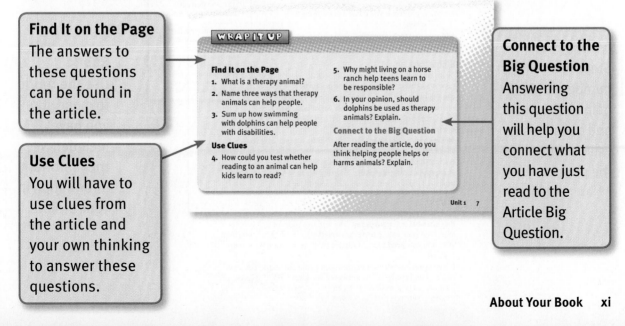

WRAP IT UP

Find It on the Page
1. What is a therapy animal?
2. Name three ways that therapy animals can help people.
3. Sum up how swimming with dolphins can help people with disabilities.

Use Clues
4. How could you test whether reading to an animal can help kids learn to read?

5. Why might living on a horse ranch help teens learn to be responsible?
6. In your opinion, should dolphins be used as therapy animals? Explain.

Connect to the Big Question
After reading the article, do you think helping people helps or harms animals? Explain.

Unit 1   7

Connect to the Big Question
Answering this question will help you connect what you have just read to the Article Big Question.

Unit Wrap Up

At the end of each unit you will find a fun project that will help you put everything you read together to answer the Unit Big Question.

Project
This is the type of project you will be doing. All activities are done with a partner or in a small group.

Page 1

Unit Articles
Use this list to pick articles that you especially enjoyed or want to think more about.

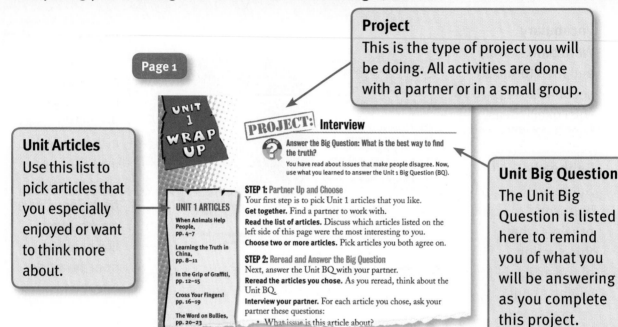

UNIT 1 WRAP UP

PROJECT: Interview

Answer the Big Question: What is the best way to find the truth?

You have read about issues that make people disagree. Now, use what you learned to answer the Unit 1 Big Question (BQ).

UNIT 1 ARTICLES

When Animals Help People, pp. 4–7

Learning the Truth in China, pp. 8–11

In the Grip of Graffiti, pp. 12–15

Cross Your Fingers! pp. 16–19

The Word on Bullies, pp. 20–23

STEP 1: Partner Up and Choose
Your first step is to pick Unit 1 articles that you like.
Get together. Find a partner to work with.
Read the list of articles. Discuss which articles listed on the left side of this page were the most interesting to you.
Choose two or more articles. Pick articles you both agree on.

STEP 2: Reread and Answer the Big Question
Next, answer the Unit BQ with your partner.
Reread the articles you chose. As you reread, think about the Unit BQ.
Interview your partner. For each article you chose, ask your partner these questions:
• What issue is this article about?

Unit Big Question
The Unit Big Question is listed here to remind you of what you will be answering as you complete this project.

Page 2

Activity Steps
Steps are numbered with helpful directions and questions to walk you through the project.

...what was true?
Do you think you made a good decision? Explain.
Add your partner's examples. Add to the interview notes. Be sure your notes have specific details.

STEP 5: Check and Fix
Next, you and your partner will look over the interview notes to see whether they could be improved.
Use the rubric. Use the rubric questions to evaluate your work. Answer each question yes or no. Then trade interview notes with your partner. Use the rubric to evaluate your partner's work, too.
Discuss your evaluations. Explain to your partner why you answered a question yes or no. For every no answer, explain what your partner could do to get a yes answer.
Improve your interview notes. If your interview notes could be improved, fix the mistakes or add more details.

STEP 6: Practice and Present
Get ready to present to your classmates.
Practice what you want to say. You will use your interview notes to explain how your partner answered the Unit BQ. Think about what you will need to say. Practice your presentation with your partner.
Present your interview notes. Introduce your partner to the class and explain how he or she answered the Unit 1 BQ. Include at least one specific example from an article and one example from your partner's own experience.

RUBRIC

Do the interview notes . . .
• include an answer to the Unit BQ?
• have the titles of at least two articles from Unit 1?
• give at least one example from each article to explain the answer to the Unit BQ?
• give at least one specific real-life example to explain the answer to the Unit BQ?

Rubric
Use the rubric to make sure you have included all the important information in your project.

Textbook Scavenger Hunt

To make the most of independent learning, you will need to use the unique features of this book on your own. Now that you have reviewed the features of this text, use this scavenger hunt to get to know your book from cover to cover.

With a partner or small group answer the questions below on your own paper. Use the walk-through on the previous pages as a quick reminder if you need it. Then share your responses with the class.

1 Turn to the Table of Contents. Scan to find an article that interests you. How can you find the article in the book? Turn to the article. What question will you answer as you read?

2 How are the topics in the index organized? Scan the index to find a topic that interests you. Then flip to an article that covers this topic. What do the captions, illustrations, and other visuals tell you about the article?

3 How many units are in the book? How can you tell? Flip through your book. Pause at the unit opener illustration you like best. How does it help you connect to the Unit Big Question?

4 Where will you find a Real-Life Connection with each article? Find one that includes a graphic organizer. What information will the graphic organizer help you to think about and organize?

5 What do the special quote features in this book look like? Find an article that features a quote. What information about the article does the quote give you?

6 Locate the glossary. Find a word that you do not know and share the definition with a friend. What other information about the word can you find in the glossary?

What is the best way to find the truth?

All the reporters saw the same trial, but their accounts of it are completely different. How can you tell which account is true? This unit explores topics that have two sides to them. As you read each article, you can decide for yourself: What is the best way to find the truth?

> If you want information you can trust, where do you go to get it? Why do you think that particular source tells the truth?

Real-Life Connection

What do you know about animals that help people? Find out by telling whether you think each idea below is true or false.

1. Animals can help people under stress to relax.
2. Petting an animal can lower a person's blood pressure.
3. Dogs can help kids learn to read better.
4. Dolphins enjoy swimming with people.

Check It Out

Service animals help people with disabilities get around. For example, guide dogs help blind people, and hearing dogs help people who cannot hear important sounds, like traffic noises. Therapy animals give a different kind of help. They help people by being friends to them. Therapy animals offer people love and support.

WORD BANK

evaluate (i VAL yuh wayt) *verb*   When you **evaluate** someone or something, you form an opinion based on what you know.
EXAMPLE: *My teacher helped me **evaluate** my writing so that I could improve my paper.*

evidence (E vuh duhns) *noun*   **Evidence** shows that something is true.
EXAMPLE: *The crumbs Mauricio left on the table were **evidence** he had eaten the last piece of pizza.*

mean (meen) *verb*   To **mean** is to show or give a sign of something.
EXAMPLE: *The buds on the tree **mean** that spring is almost here!*

perceive (puhr SEEV) *verb*   When you **perceive** something, you notice it or understand it.
EXAMPLE: *I did not **perceive** that it was raining until a drop of rain fell on my nose.*

reality (ree A luh tee) *noun*   **Reality** is made up of things that exist in the real world.
EXAMPLE: *To escape from **reality,** Jennifer reads comic books and plays fantasy games on her computer.*

THE BIG ?

What is the best way to find the truth?

Dogs and cats are used in hospitals and other places to cheer people up and make them feel better. Some wild animals are used to help people, too. As you read the article, ask yourself: **Does helping people help or harm animals?**

WHEN ANIMALS HELP PEOPLE

Picture a horse ranch in Montana. Troubled kids from the city have been sent there to live. In the city, they started fights. Some of them also shoplifted and used drugs. Now, far from the **reality** of city life, they are riding and taking care of horses. For the first time, the kids are learning to be responsible. The horses need them—and they need the horses.

▲ Horses are sometimes used as therapy animals.

Now picture a pool in Florida. In the pool are young people who cannot walk or who have other disabilities. They splash happily in the water as large dolphins swim and roll around them. The kids smile as they pet the dolphins. The dolphins seem to be smiling, too. Does that **mean** the dolphins are happy?

ANIMAL THERAPY WORKS Animal therapy is not a new idea. For years, pets have helped people in hospitals and nursing homes. Health experts say therapy with animals helps people relax. **Evidence** shows that people can lower their blood pressure by petting animals. It also shows that people's moods can improve when they are with animals.

Therapy animals can help kids in the classroom, too. Students who have trouble reading may not want to read in front of other kids. Reading aloud to a dog, on the other hand, is fun. After all, a dog does not **perceive** mistakes or **evaluate** how well someone reads. One dog trainer believes that young people who read to dogs feel better about themselves. As a teacher once said to her, "The world is truly a better place with the love of therapy dogs to help kids read."

Experts even believe that animals can help kids with emotional problems. Some kids have never been loved. When they feel the love of an animal, they may learn to return the feeling. In time, kids may learn to have positive feelings for people, too.

Kids who have trouble communicating may also benefit from animal therapy. Some of them find it hard to talk to people but easy to talk to dogs and cats. It builds kids' confidence when they tell a dog to do a trick and the dog does it. That confidence can give kids the courage to talk to people, too.

Animals also help older people who are lonely and out of touch with **reality.** Helping to care for an animal makes their lives more **meaningful.** They pay more attention to the world around them. They look forward to visits from their animal friends.

GOOD FOR ANIMALS?

Evidently, being a therapy animal may be good for the animal, also. Dogs, cats, horses, and other animals need care and love. Therapy animals get plenty of attention.

But is being a therapy animal good for all animals? Some animal rights groups say no. These groups believe that being a therapy animal may be harmful to wild animals, such as dolphins.

▲
Dolphins may not like living in a tank of water.

Over the past thirty years, dolphins have been used to help people with disabilities—especially young people. Some of the kids have serious emotional problems. Others need wheelchairs to get around. Getting into the water with dolphins and their trainers makes the kids feel happy and free.

The dolphins, on the other hand, probably do not feel free. They are used to living in the ocean. Living in a pool may make them feel trapped. Though people **perceive** the look on a dolphin's face to be a smile, this **perception** is probably wrong. Living with people can upset dolphins. They may act out by bumping and pushing people. Some dolphins try to hurt themselves. Being therapy animals may even shorten dolphins' lives.

Many people agree that animal therapy can be good for animals and people alike. Other people, however, argue that it is wrong to use dolphins for therapy. "There is no real **evidence** that dolphins can heal us," says one animal rights spokesperson. Dolphins that are forced to live in tanks of water "can't even heal themselves," he says.

WRAP IT UP

Find It on the Page

1. What is a therapy animal?

2. Name three ways that therapy animals can help people.

3. Sum up how swimming with dolphins can help people with disabilities.

Use Clues

4. How could you test whether reading to an animal can help kids learn to read?

5. Why might living on a horse ranch help teens learn to be responsible?

6. In your opinion, should dolphins be used as therapy animals? Explain.

Connect to the Big Question

After reading the article, do you think helping people helps or harms animals? Explain.

Real-Life Connection

How much do you know about the Internet, search engines, and censorship? Rate your knowledge on a chart like the one below.

Idea	Know a Lot	Know a Little	Know Nothing
The Internet			
Search Engines			
Censorship			

Check It Out

To *censor* information means to keep it from being known. Some governments censor certain facts or events. They think this information could be dangerous for the people they rule to know.

For example, in China, the government controls Internet search engines like Google and Yahoo. The Chinese government is not a democracy. In China, the government—not the people—decides on its own what the people's rights are.

WORD BANK

awareness (uh WER nuhs) *noun*   **Awareness** is knowing that something, such as a problem, exists.
EXAMPLE: *Watching the news gives you an **awareness** of local and world events.*

explain (ik SPLAYN) *verb*   If you **explain** something, you give reasons for it or make it clear.
EXAMPLE: *Lindsay asked her parents to **explain** why she couldn't watch the movie.*

factual (FAK chuh wuhl) *adjective*   Something that is **factual** is real or true.
EXAMPLE: *News reports are supposed to be **factual**.*

observe (uhb ZUHRV) *verb*   To **observe** something is to watch it carefully.
EXAMPLE: *Scientists **observe** animals to learn about their behaviors in the wild.*

reveal (ri VEEL) *verb*   When you **reveal** something, you uncover or show something that was hidden.
EXAMPLE: *We will **reveal** the winner after this message.*

What is the best way to find the truth?

In the United States, you can go to the library or use the Internet to get information on most subjects. You can even find information that goes against the national government. In some nations, the government censors information. As you read the article, ask yourself: **How does the country in which you live affect the information that you can find?**

Learning the Truth in China

Teens in China do not have the same access to information as teens in the United States do. ▼

Do you know how to "google"? That's a word people use a lot today. It means "to search for information." The word comes from an Internet search engine called Google. When you google a topic, the program will usually **reveal** thousands of Web sites to find more information about that topic.

If you google *democracy,* you get more than 77 million results. At least, if you live in the United States, you do. In Iran, Vietnam, or China, you could google the word *democracy* and get only a few results, if any. The governments of these countries keep tight control over some **factual** information.

CENSORING THE INTERNET Imagine you wrote a letter and posted it to the Internet. You wanted others to read it and talk about it. Then imagine trying to check the letter the next day. Instead of the letter, you get a message that says you are not allowed to see your letter.

Worse yet, you see nothing at all. It has simply disappeared! That is what sometimes happens in China.

In 1998, the Chinese government decided it needed to censor the Internet. Controlling newspapers and television was not enough to manage the information people were allowed to receive. If the government really wanted to control information, officials needed to **observe** information on the Internet, too. The part of the government responsible for watching the Internet is called the Golden Shield Project. The Golden Shield Project looks for information the government believes is harmful. The Project searches the Internet for sites that use key words like *democracy, freedom, justice,* and *human rights.* The government blocks these sites so that no one in China can view them. In some cases, the government may simply pull the sites off the Internet.

> **The Project searches for key words like *democracy*.**

The Golden Shield Project cannot work on its own. Companies who own search engines must agree to block information that the Chinese government wants to hide. U.S. companies **explain** that they block this information because it is the only way for them to do business in China. Some groups, however, argue that these companies should refuse to do business with China. The groups believe that the government would be forced to change.

LIVING WITH CENSORSHIP If you lived in China and used the Internet to find **facts** about a topic, you might see Internet police cartoon character Jingjing or Chacha and an **explanation** that the information you want is not allowed. More likely, you would not get any search results at all. You might think that information about your topic does not exist.

The government's efforts to censor information do not always work, however. People are **aware** of the censors and work to get around them. Sometimes a Web site posts information even though it is not allowed. People see the stories before the government removes them from the Internet. Often, people pass along important information by word of mouth until it is well known. Other Web sites use blank spaces in place of words that the Golden Shield Project looks for. Then the sites do not get blocked. Some companies are working to create software to help people in countries like China access blocked Web sites. One Chinese student commented, "The more the government tries to prevent the Chinese from learning something, the more they will want to do it."

LOOKING FORWARD More and more people are working to allow equal access to information. In January of 2007, students, teachers, human rights groups, and businesses like Microsoft, Google, and Yahoo attended an important meeting. They gathered to create guidelines to bring a new **awareness** of human rights to the Internet.

As the Internet continues to grow, more and more people use it to post facts and opinions. It is becoming harder for the Chinese government to censor knowledge. Chinese people now have their own versions of MySpace, instant messaging, and chatrooms. For now, the government is **observing** these sites carefully. Businesses might be able to change the way the government controls these tools.

WRAP IT UP

Find It on the Page

1. What has the word *google* come to mean?

2. What key words are often blocked from Internet research in China? Why?

3. Why have the owners of search engines like Google and Yahoo agreed to censor themselves?

Use Clues

4. In your opinion, why does the Chinese government use cartoon characters to help police the Internet?

5. Do you think efforts to open up the Internet in China will be successful? Why or why not?

6. Do you think that Chinese students are more motivated to get information than are students in other countries? Why or why not?

Connect to the Big Question

Now that you have read the article, how do you think the country in which you live affects the information you can find?

Real-Life Connection

You have probably seen graffiti—pictures or words that people draw or write, without permission, on walls or other things. What comes to mind when you think of graffiti? Make a word web like the one below. Use it to write your ideas.

Graffiti

ugly pictures

WORD BANK

conclude (kuhn KLOOD) *verb*   To **conclude** is to use clues to figure out something that is not directly stated.
EXAMPLE: *After discovering that his wallet was empty, Cameron had to **conclude** that he could not go to the movies.*

debate (di BAYT) *verb*   When you **debate,** you argue about something by giving reasons for it or against it.
EXAMPLE: *I had to **debate** other family members when we disagreed about what to do for our vacation.*

evaluate (i VAL yuh wayt) *verb*   When you **evaluate** someone or something, you form an opinion based on what you know.
EXAMPLE: *Latricia asked her brother to **evaluate** her report to see whether it was OK.*

perceive (puhr SEEV) *verb*   When you **perceive** something, you notice it or understand it.
EXAMPLE: *Just by looking at her, I could **perceive** how angry she was.*

strategy (STRA tuh jee) *noun*   A **strategy** is a set of plans for doing something well.
EXAMPLE: *My coach taught me a new **strategy** for successfully catching a football.*

What is the best way to find the truth?

Two people look at graffiti on a wall. One says, "That's really ugly." The other says, "Bare walls are uglier. Those drawings are art." What do you think of graffiti? As you read the article, ask yourself: **Is graffiti art, or is it damage to property?**

In the Grip of Graffiti

Suppose you are a good artist. You like to paint with bright colors, and you like to paint on empty spaces outside, like walls and doors. You **evaluate** your work and think it is wonderful. Now suppose you walk outside one morning and find your home covered with graffiti. Would you **conclude** that that was wonderful, too?

People have written and drawn on walls for thousands of years. For just as long, people have complained about the markings. However, what we call graffiti today first appeared in New York City in the late 1960s. Young people sprayed paint on walls and sidewalks in their neighborhoods. They signed their nicknames. The first graffiti makers were people with names such as TOP CAT 126, Joe 182, and Julio 204. These young people called their work "tagging."

Tagging spread in the early 1970s. That is when a messenger—Taki 183—began to tag subway cars in which he traveled. In 1971, the *New York Times* wrote about Taki 183. The newspaper used the word *graffiti* to describe what he did.

▲
How do you feel about this graffiti?

By the early 1980s, graffiti covered everything from trains to buildings to statues in New York City. The work of one artist in particular caught people's attention. Keith Haring, an art student, began making drawings in subway stations. Workers had used black paper to cover walls waiting for ads. Haring thought the black paper would be a good place for art, so he set chalk to paper. Soon he had made hundreds of pictures. Many people liked them.

People began to **debate** whether graffiti could actually be art. Artists such as Jean-Michel Basquiat began making graffiti-style paintings. Art galleries sold the work of Basquiat and other artists like him for thousands of dollars.

DANGEROUS AND COSTLY Meanwhile, other people began to **perceive** graffiti as a big problem. In some areas, taggers sprayed street signs until nobody could read them. In New York City, taggers covered whole subway cars. Passengers could not see out of windows or read station signs.

Families had to pay to have graffiti removed from their property. Business owners hired people to clean graffiti from their buildings. Cities had to pay to clean graffiti from bridges, tunnel walls, and statues.

Graffiti cleanup is still very expensive. The chart below shows how much several cities spent to remove graffiti in 2006. Graffiti costs people money in other ways, also. In areas with a lot of graffiti, stores do less business. The value of houses goes down, too.

THE HIGH COST OF GRAFFITI		
Name of City	**Population in 2006**	**Amount Spent (in $)**
San Jose, California	1,000,000	2,000,000
Pittsburgh, Pennsylvania	300,000	350,000
Omaha, Nebraska	400,000	100,000
Denver, Colorado	550,000	1,000,000
Milwaukee, Wisconsin	550,000	1,000,000
Chicago, Illinois	2,800,000	6,500,000

Information is from Graffitihurts.org.

WHY DO THEY DO IT? Drawing or writing on property without the owner's permission is against the law. So why does it continue? There is no single answer. Many taggers, like Taki 183, use tagging to let people know who they are and where they have been.

Other graffiti makers use graffiti to spread ideas about politics, life, and society. For example, graffiti makers sprayed "Save our jobs!" on buildings in a neighborhood where many businesses had closed.

For still other graffiti makers, painting pictures is a **strategy** for showing off their talent. Some of these would-be artists believe they are making cities more colorful places to live. As one graffiti maker put it, "Sure, painting on someone's house or writing your name on a wall is not a good thing, but you're saying you'd rather live in a metropolis grey-walled city housing with nothing but narrow-minded robotic people."

Given the problems that graffiti causes, however, some people have come to the **conclusion** that it does not really matter whether graffiti is art. When someone writes or draws on property without permission, it's a crime. That is one thing about graffiti that is *not* **debatable.**

WRAP IT UP

Find It on the Page

1. What is tagging?

2. List three problems graffiti can cause.

3. List three ways that graffiti use could be considered positive.

Use Clues

4. Why might a store in a graffiti-free area do more business than a store in an area that has a lot of graffiti?

5. What advice would you give to cities that want to stop graffiti? Explain.

6. What do you think of graffiti, and why?

Connect to the Big Question

Did the article make you change your mind about whether graffiti is art or property damage? Explain your answer.

Real-Life Connection

Do you think it is bad luck to break a mirror? Have you ever crossed your fingers for luck? These actions are examples of superstitions. What other superstitions do you know? List them on a chart like the one below.

Things That Are Lucky	Things That Are Unlucky
four-leaf clover	Friday the thirteenth

believable (buh LEE vuh buhl) *adjective*   When something is **believable,** it seems possible or true.
EXAMPLE: *Gerald's excuse for being late to school was **believable,** so he did not get into trouble.*

explain (ik SPLAYN) *verb*   If you **explain** something, you give reasons for it or make it clear.
EXAMPLE: *My dad will **explain** the steps for fixing a bicycle.*

factual (FAK chuh wuhl) *adjective*   Something that is **factual** is real or true.
EXAMPLE: *To find out when cars were first invented, look in an encyclopedia for a **factual** article about them.*

fiction (FIK shuhn) *noun*   **Fiction** is writing or ideas that come from the imagination rather than real life.
EXAMPLE: *Comic books and short stories are examples of **fiction**.*

view (vyoo) *noun*   Your **view** of something is your opinion of it.
EXAMPLE: *Claire's **view** of baseball is that it is the most boring game in the world.*

What is the best way to find the truth?

Are bad things more likely to happen on Friday the thirteenth than on Tuesday the tenth? Is it bad luck to break a mirror? Why do some people think that wearing certain clothes will bring them good luck? As you read the article, ask yourself: Is there any truth to superstitions?

Cross Your Fingers!

Do you want to get an A on your next math test? Rub a rabbit's foot before you take the test. Good luck will come your way. Say good-bye to that A if you walk under a ladder, though. Everyone knows walking there is bad luck.

Chances are that this advice sounds **unbelievably** silly to you. People today tend to think of superstitions as a kind of **fiction.** Long ago, however, people took superstitions very seriously. In fact, the word *superstition* comes from a life-and-death situation. Soldiers in ancient Rome who lived through battles were called superstitians, or "those standing above." They were called this because they stood above soldiers who lay dead on the battlefield. Over time, *superstition* became linked in people's minds to luck, both good and bad.

HOW SUPERSTITIONS STARTED Hundreds of years ago, living well and staying healthy seemed to be matters of luck. People did not always have enough food. They did not know how diseases started or spread. Many people died young. No one knew what caused natural events, such as storms and earthquakes.

Could this cat bring you good luck?

As a result, people looked for ways to **explain** events they did not understand. The **explanations** were not **factual,** of course. They made the world seem a much less frightening place, though. Parents passed the **beliefs** on to their children. As years passed, most people from the same culture, or group, knew the superstitions. They no longer knew, however, why and how the superstitions started.

Do you know why a rabbit's foot is sometimes thought to be lucky? Long ago, people noted that they saw wild rabbits most often in spring, when the weather grew warm. Rabbits had many babies. The animals were good food, and there were plenty of them. For these reasons, people began to think of rabbits as a sign of good health. It is not too much of a leap to see why some people began to carry a rabbit's foot for good luck.

One basketball player never plays without a rubber band around his wrist.

Other animals are considered both lucky and unlucky. While some people now **view** black cats as unlucky, people in ancient Egypt **believed** cats were sacred. A person who killed a cat could face death for doing so. Other superstitions show cats bringing good luck. One superstition says that if a cat sneezes on a bride's wedding day, she will have a happy life.

Long ago, many people **believed** in evil spirits. They worried that the invisible spirits would fly into a person's mouth when the person sneezed. To chase away the evil, people said, "Bless you."

Crossing fingers was another way to chase away evil. People believed bad luck could be trapped at the point where two fingers meet. So when people crossed their fingers, they thought they were keeping bad luck from escaping and causing harm.

SUPERSTITION IN SPORTS Though most people today laugh at superstitions, other people find them quite **believable.** In fact, some of the most superstitious people are also some of the luckiest—professional athletes.

Sports are filled with superstitious players. One basketball player never plays without a rubber band around his left wrist. Another player wore the same floppy sweat socks for every game in college and the pros.

Baseball players are superstitious, too. In the 1980s and 1990s, for example, Wade Boggs was one of baseball's greatest hitters. Boggs made sure he woke up at exactly the same time every day—7:17. He ate chicken before every game. He took batting practice at 5:17 before every game. Every time he came to bat, he drew the same shape in the dirt—a good luck symbol. In 2005, he was elected to the Baseball Hall of Fame. Did superstitions bring him luck?

GOOD LUCK OR HARD WORK? Most people would probably say Boggs succeeded because of hard work and skill. Boggs seems to have thought otherwise, though. The thing about superstitions is that if you think something makes you lucky, you become more confident. The more confident you are, the more likely you are to succeed. Maybe that's what Tryon Edwards, a philosopher, meant when he said, "Superstitions are the shadows of great truths."

WRAP IT UP

Find It on the Page

1. Who were the *superstitians*?

2. List three things that are supposed to bring bad luck.

3. Summarize how rabbits became signs of good luck.

Use Clues

4. In your opinion, why are some people still superstitious, even though superstitions are probably not true?

5. How could you prove that a superstition is true or false?

6. Do you agree that believing you are lucky can help you succeed? Explain.

Connect to the Big Question

Do you think there is any truth to superstitions? Explain.

Real-Life Connection

Imagine this situation. Every day on the way to the lunchroom, you see a big kid push a smaller kid. You feel sick when the big kid laughs as the smaller kid falls against the lockers. You hear the cruel talk, too. The big kid teases the smaller kid and dares the kid to fight back. You know the big kid is nothing but a bully. You want to help, but you are scared of the bully, too. What would you do about this situation? Why? Make a chart like the one below. Jot down your ideas on it.

What I Would Do	Why I Would Do That
I would . . .	I would do that because . . .

WORD BANK

awareness (uh WER nuhs) *noun*   **Awareness** is knowing that something, such as a problem, exists.
EXAMPLE: *My science class gave me an **awareness** of the problems that pollution can cause.*

consequence (KAHN suh kwens) *noun*   A **consequence** is a result or an outcome.
EXAMPLE: *In my family, punishment is the **consequence** of breaking rules.*

evidence (E vuh duhns) *noun*   **Evidence** shows that something is true.
EXAMPLE: *You don't need to be a firefighter to know that smoke and heat are **evidence** of a fire.*

pattern (PA tuhrn) *noun*   A **pattern** is a habit, or way of behaving that does not change.
EXAMPLE: *Every morning, Ed follows the same **pattern:** get up, get dressed, eat breakfast, and leave the house by seven A.M.*

truth (trooth) *noun*   **Truth** is something that is correct and supported by facts.
EXAMPLE: *When the phone bill came, my mom knew the **truth** about the number of calls I made.*

What is the best way to find the truth?

What should you do if a bully picks on you? Fighting back is not smart. Running away may only make the bully bolder. There is nothing worse than being bullied—or is there? Maybe it is worse to be a bully. As you read the article, ask yourself: What is the truth about bullies?

THE WORD ON BULLIES

They grab your shirt. They take your lunch money. They use words like fists to hurt you. If you act afraid, they laugh in your face. Sometimes they make other kids join in the cruel laughter. You know who "they" are: bullies.

Bullying is a common problem. Many young people know the scary feeling of facing a bully who wants to hurt them. The bullying could be a push or a grab, but it could also be a word or an e-mail. The **truth** is that bullying happens in many ways.

Physical bullying is hitting, kicking, or pushing someone. Taking someone's school supplies—that is physical bullying, too. Threatening to do such things is also a form of physical bullying.

Verbal bullying is using words to make other people feel bad. Sometimes it is called talking trash.

▲
Refusing to talk to a friend is a form of bullying.

This kind of bullying includes calling someone names, teasing the person, or being insulting—whether face-to-face or in e-mails or instant messages.

There is another kind of bullying. Sometimes a person decides to stop speaking to a friend without saying why. Freezing out a friend, spreading rumors, and gossiping are relationship bullying.

WHY KIDS BULLY Bullies seem tough. As a **consequence,** some kids think bullies are strong and confident. However, the opposite is likely to be **true.** Most bullies **truly** do not like themselves. Making other people feel bad makes bullies feel good.

Another reason that kids bully is to get attention. People usually want positive attention. Bullies may not know how to get positive attention, however. **Consequently,** they settle for any kind of attention they can get.

Bullying may even run in someone's family. Some kids learn to pick on others because older brothers or sisters or parents picked on them. When people grow up being bullied at home, they follow the only **pattern** they know. They think that the only way to be grown-up and powerful is to pick on someone who seems weaker.

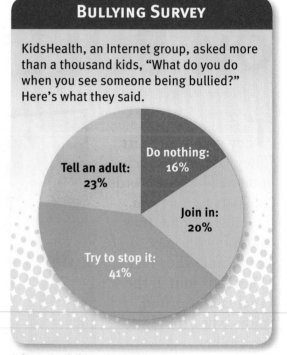

BULLYING SURVEY

KidsHealth, an Internet group, asked more than a thousand kids, "What do you do when you see someone being bullied?" Here's what they said.

Do nothing: 16%
Join in: 20%
Try to stop it: 41%
Tell an adult: 23%

Information is from KidsHealth.org.

WHAT YOU CAN DO Some young people feel helpless when they see bullying. In fact, 16 percent of kids who took part in a recent survey said they do nothing at all when they see someone being bullied. (See the pie chart for more results.) It does not have to be that way. You have the power to stop bullies. Take steps to stop bullying.

Speak Firmly   If a bully bothers you, stand up straight. Talk back in a firm voice. Make eye contact. Tell the bully to bother someone else.

Seek Help   Lots of adults can help you solve the problem of bullying. The most important thing you can do is raise **awareness.** Speak up and make an adult **aware** of the problem. If someone sends you a threatening e-mail, keep it as **evidence.** Show it to an adult.

Stay Calm   The words a bully says can make you feel like crying or getting angry and yelling. That is just what the bully wants you to do. Instead, you should stay calm and ignore the bully. When you walk away without a word, you take the bully's power away.

Stick Together   There are also actions you can take to protect yourself from bullying. Go with a friend or a group of kids to school and other places. Avoid places that are not supervised by adults. Bullies are not brave. When they are outnumbered, they usually give up.

Experts say that almost 4 million kids across the United States are bullies. Chances are good that you know one of them. Now that you have learned more about the problem, you can be a part of the solution. "This is how I deal with bullies," says Sydney, a middle school student. "I leave it alone, or I tell someone who is in charge."

WRAP IT UP

Find It on the Page

1. Give two examples of physical bullying.

2. What are two other kinds of bullying?

3. Describe two things you could do if someone tried to bully you.

Use Clues

4. Why do people sometimes think that bullies are tough and confident?

5. If you were the school principal, how would you solve the problem of bullying?

6. Do you think the article gives good advice about how to stop bullies? Explain why or why not.

Connect to the Big Question

After reading the article, what do you think is the real truth about bullies? Explain.

Real-Life Connection

What do you know about peace camps? On a chart like the one below, rate how well you understand basic things about peace camps.

Idea	Know a Lot	Know a Little	Know Nothing
What peace camps are			
Who goes to peace camp			
What campers learn			

Check It Out

The Middle Eastern lands of Israel and Palestine have a long history of conflict. People of Palestine believe that Israel unfairly took some of their land. People of Israel argue that the land is theirs. Religious differences have also caused problems.

WORD BANK

convince (kuhn VINS) *verb*   When you **convince** someone of something, you make the person feel sure about it.
EXAMPLE: *After my school began charging more money for lunch, I was able to* **convince** *my dad to raise my allowance.*

debate (di BAYT) *verb*   When you **debate,** you argue about something by giving reasons for it or against it.
EXAMPLE: *This afternoon in student council, we will* **debate** *the idea of wearing uniforms to school.*

fiction (FIK shuhn) *noun*   **Fiction** is writing or ideas that come from the imagination rather than from real life.
EXAMPLE: *The idea that a person could travel to the moon once seemed like* **fiction.**

insight (IN syt) *noun*   When you have **insight** into an idea or a problem, you understand it clearly.
EXAMPLE: *My history class gave me* **insight** *into cultural differences.*

reveal (ri VEEL) *verb*   When you **reveal** something, you uncover or show something that was hidden.
EXAMPLE: *Mom opened the curtains to* **reveal** *the sunshine.*

What is the best way to find the truth?

When two groups are at war, they consider each other the enemy. They think only about the differences that divide them. People who have never even met hate each other. Peace camps try to change these attitudes. As you read the article, ask yourself: What is the best way to understand people who are different?

Campers Give Peace a Chance

Bloodshed is all some children have ever known. In some places in the Middle East, for example, violence is part of everyday life. Peace seems like a dream or **fiction** to young people who live there.

Though many of these people have never met people on the other side, they have learned to hate and fear them. Differences in beliefs and values have **convinced** these kids that they and the others are enemies.

Some groups in the United States would like to change this. These groups bring together kids from lands that do not get along such as Israel and Palestine. The groups pay for the kids to travel to the United States and attend peace camp together.

Two popular peace camps are the Middle East Peace Camp for Children—in Seattle, Washington—and Seeds of Peace—in Otisfield, Maine. These camps offer the usual kinds of fun. Campers play sports and do arts and crafts.

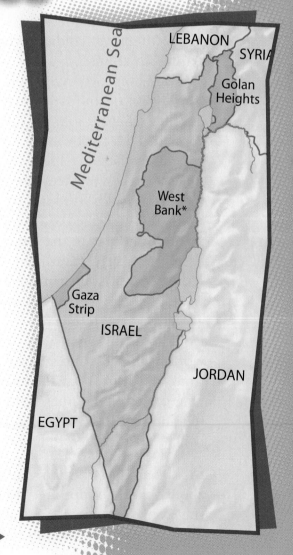

Israel and Palestine are neighbors. They share the same border. ▶

Campers also learn how to solve problems. They learn to respect and understand people who are different from them. Camp gives them **insight** into one another.

At first, the campers who go to peace camp may be afraid of one another. They have learned to fear people from groups their group has fought. One young camper from Palestine **revealed** his feelings when he said, "I was afraid to introduce myself because that person might be Israeli and the picture I had of them was soldiers who wanted to kill us."

Back home, young people from Palestine and Israel may have few chances to meet one another. That is true even when they live only a few miles apart. As one teenager from Israel said, "It's kind of funny that you need to take a plane all the way to the United States to meet a Palestinian girl who lives twenty minutes away." Though campers travel a long way just to meet, most would probably agree it is

▲
Kids learn about each other by playing sports together at peace camp.

worth it. Peace camp lets them get to know one another. For the first time, they learn that "the enemy" has a name and a face.

Each camper comes from a land where most people have similar religious beliefs. As a result, many campers have never learned about beliefs that differ from theirs. Camp gives them the chance to learn.

ENEMIES BECOME FRIENDS Campers learn how they can help bring about peace. Groups meet to talk about how to work together. They stay away from discussions about the history or politics of a place. They look toward the future instead of the past.

Counselors at peace camps help campers learn from one another. Kids talk about the problems that divide them. They **debate** issues and listen to the other side of an argument. The group discussions take place over several weeks. It takes time for people to **reveal** what they truly believe and feel.

Campers do not try to **convince** one another that one side or the other is right. The point is to talk out their problems. They learn to listen to each other. They try to understand.

THE KEY TO UNDERSTANDING Campers have fun playing soccer and softball. Sports are fun, but they are also a way to learn how to work together as a team. Campers learn that they can get along. Differences begin to fade away. Kids come to see that many of the ideas they had about one another are **fiction,** not reality.

In fact, campers learn that they are more alike than different. This **revelation** is key to solving the problems between their peoples. If fighting is to end, each side must learn to understand the other.

The experiences campers have make them more **insightful** about their peoples' problems. The hope is that they will be able to imagine a different, better kind of life when they go home and become older. "Here, you see it work," says one camper. "You see it can be possible."

WRAP IT UP

Find It on the Page

1. What is a peace camp?

2. What kinds of things do young people do at peace camp?

3. Why do campers fear each other before they even meet?

Use Clues

4. How might the lessons that campers learn at peace camp help kids in the United States?

5. How do you think sports helps people understand each other?

6. What is your opinion of having peace camps in the United States? Explain.

Connect to the Big Question

After reading the article, what do you think is the best way to understand people who are different?

Real-Life Connection

What do you know about child soldiers? Use a Word Web like the one below to see whether you can answer any of the questions listed.

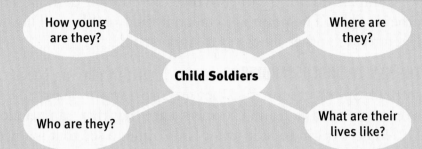

How young are they?

Where are they?

Child Soldiers

Who are they?

What are their lives like?

Check It Out

Refugees are people who leave their countries because of war or natural disasters like an earthquake. Displaced people are refugees who leave their homes but have not left their country. Child refugees in some countries at war are forced to become soldiers.

WORD BANK

affect (uh FEKT) *verb* To **affect** something is to create a change in it.
EXAMPLE: *The referee's decision will **affect** the outcome of the game.*

conclude (kuhn KLOOD) *verb* To **conclude** is to use clues to figure something out that is not directly stated.
EXAMPLE: *When Evelyn woke up on the couch, she had to **conclude** that she had dozed off while reading.*

reality (ree A luh tee) *noun* **Reality** is made up of things that exist in the real world.
EXAMPLE: *The team's losing record is an unpleasant **reality**.*

truth (trooth) *noun* **Truth** is something that is correct and supported by facts.
EXAMPLE: *Francine asked Phil to stop lying and to tell her the **truth**.*

What is the best way to find the truth?

A young boy is forced to be a soldier in a war between rebels and the government of his country. Is he responsible for the terrible things he does during war? Can he become a normal kid when the war ends? As you read the article, ask yourself: **How do events in our lives shape the truth of who we are?**

RETURN TO HUMANITY

When Ishmael Beah was young, he did not carry books to school. Instead, he carried guns to war. His **reality** was very different from that of most kids around the world. Beah was twelve when war broke out. In Sierra Leone, Beah's homeland in West Africa, rebels fought government forces for power. Beah and millions of other people were trapped in the middle of a terrible war. No one in Sierra Leone expected society to fall apart so completely. Once, people in that country truly welcomed strangers. Then war tore the country apart.

Beah went from dancing to American rap music to running for his life. His family was wiped out. He and other children hid in the forest. After a year of hiding, the government's army captured them. It forced Beah to become a soldier and fight in the war.

Soldiers are often forced to do terrible things. Beah was only thirteen, though, and the experiences of war **affect** the young very strongly. He still has nightmares about that time. Beah says, "People don't believe that other human beings can lose their humanity to such an extent."

▲ **Sierra Leone was torn apart by war.**

Beah was eventually able to leave Sierra Leone. He came to the United States, where he attended college. Beah now speaks out about the problems of child refugees and soldiers.

MILLIONS OF CHILD REFUGEES The terrible **truth** is that Beah was only one of millions of children around the world who became refugees. In Africa alone, seven countries have had civil wars in the past ten years. Today, about 100,000 children are involved in wars in Africa. Most of the children are eight to ten years old.

In Africa, more than 300,000 boys and girls under age eighteen are soldiers. Many are under age ten. In some places, the rule is that anyone as tall as a rifle is old enough to carry one.

Ishmael Beah inspires others with his life story.

INVISIBLE WOUNDS Not all child soldiers are injured in battle. Beah, for one, was not wounded. But experts say nearly all suffer true emotional harm. Scientists studied nearly 300 former child soldiers who fought in El Salvador's civil war in the 1980s. Even ten years after the civil war ended, many still had feelings of fear, anxiety, and hopelessness.

The study in El Salvador **concluded** that former child soldiers need help in order to live normal lives. They need food, shelter, and job training. More important, they need to talk about the terrible things they saw and did. They need support from their communities and time to heal.

HOPE FOR THE FUTURE Beah and others, like the United Nations High Commission for Refugees (UNHCR), hope to make people want to help save child refugees. The UNHCR has people working in trouble spots around the world. The group's goal is to provide safe choices for displaced children. Recently, sixty-six nations agreed to stop forcing people under the age of eighteen to be soldiers. The United Nations Children's Fund (UNICEF), Human Rights Watch, and other groups work to rescue children serving in armies.

Beah believes that child soldiers can return to normal life. He spent months in a United Nations rehabilitation center. There, he learned right from wrong all over again. He got job training and social support. His personal story and the studies of UNICEF and other groups are **conclusive.** They show that violence and war change children. With help, however, even child soldiers can overcome their past. They can grow up to lead good lives and learn to be kind to other people.

"I lost my humanity," says Ishmael Beah. "Everyone can lose their humanity if they're put in the circumstance that I was. I needed to explain the **reality** of what happens, how children become like this. That's the only thing they know."

WRAP IT UP

Find It on the Page

1. How old was Ishmael Beah when war broke out in his country?

2. How did Beah end up as a soldier?

3. How did war change life in Sierra Leone?

Use Clues

4. What conclusions can you draw about how war changes child soldiers, even many years after they have stopped fighting?

5. What might happen to former child soldiers who try to ignore their past?

6. What do you think would be the worst thing about being a refugee?

Connect to the Big Question

After reading the article, do you think events in our lives shape the truth of who we are? If so, how much do they shape it?

Real-Life Connection

Luol Deng is a professional basketball player who not only plays basketball, but also finds ways to help people in the country where he grew up. The author of the article you are about to read says that some people look up to Deng for his heart, not his height. What does it mean to look up to someone for his or her heart? Do you know people whom you look up to because of their heart? Write your thoughts on your own paper before you read the article.

Check It Out

Basketball player Luol Deng is from Sudan, a country in northeastern Africa. In the 1980s, civil war broke out in Sudan. Thousands of people were killed. Millions had to leave their homes. They moved into refugee camps in Sudan. In these "tent cities," refugees can live with less of a threat of being killed.

WORD BANK

believable (buh LEE vuh buhl) *adjective*   When something is **believable,** it seems possible or true.
EXAMPLE: *The short story that Ed wrote was so **believable,** I thought the events actually happened!*

convince (kuhn VINS) *verb*   When you **convince** someone of something, you make the person feel sure about it.
EXAMPLE: *Though Felicia didn't want to go to the party, I was able to **convince** her to go by telling her Joe was going, too.*

insight (IN syt) *noun*   When you have **insight** into an idea or a problem, you understand it clearly.
EXAMPLE: *Babysitting has given me **insight** into what it might be like to be a parent.*

rarely (RAYR lee) *adverb*   Something that **rarely** happens does not happen often.
EXAMPLE: *My grandmother lives so far away that I **rarely** get to see her.*

report (ri PAWRT) *noun*   A **report** gives information about a subject.
EXAMPLE: *Caryn's book **report** about A Wrinkle in Time was so interesting that it made me want to read the book.*

What is the best way to find the truth?

Luol Deng is a basketball star. When he is on the court, thousands of fans cheer for him. When he is off the court, people cheer for him for very different reasons. As you read the article, ask yourself: How has Deng's past made him the true winner he is today?

Luol Deng: A True Winner

Luol Deng races down the basketball court. Looking back, he signals to a teammate dribbling the ball. Quick as a cat, Deng leaps toward the basket. His teammate fires the ball high above the rim. The ball and Deng meet in mid-air, and he shouts as he slams the ball through the net. What an **unbelievable** dunk! Fans go wild. After the game, parents do not need to **convince** their kids to ask for Deng's autograph. The kids look up to the 6-foot 9-inch-tall Deng as they wait for him to sign his name.

Meanwhile, thousands of miles away, families go to sleep in a crowded refugee camp, wrapped in a different kind of net. They know little about Deng's basketball skills. People in the refugee camp **rarely** hear a news **report** about the United States. The people do know, however, that Deng has helped them get mosquito nets to keep them safe from disease. Like U.S. basketball fans, they look up to Deng. But they look up to him for his heart, not his height.

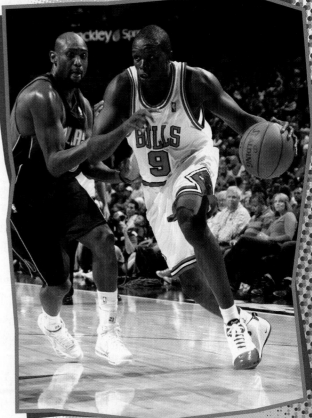

▲ Luol Deng is a strong player on the court.

If you are a basketball fan, you probably know about Deng, the forward for the Chicago Bulls. In high school, he was one of the top players in the United States. After graduation, he became an all-American college player. Then, in 2004, he became a pro with the Bulls. Deng is **believed** to be one of the best young players in the National Basketball Association (NBA).

A DIFFICULT LIFE Today, life is good for Deng. He earns more than 2 million dollars a year playing a game he loves. Fans love him. Life was not always so good for Deng, though. When he was a child, his life was filled with the sound of gunfire and screams of terror.

Many refugees live in camps along the border between Sudan and Chad.

Deng was born in Sudan. His father served in the government until war tore apart the country. Bullets and bombs drove Deng's family out of Sudan. They moved to England. At age fourteen, Deng came to the United States to go to high school—and to play basketball.

HELPING HIS HOMELAND Deng has lived in several countries since he and his family left Sudan. Still, his heart remains with the people of his homeland. Unlike Deng, however, these people cannot afford to move to faraway countries. They are forced to live in crowded refugee camps.

Deng has helped people in Sudan as a spokesperson for a group called Nothing but Nets. The group raises money to buy mosquito netting for people in African refugee camps. More than 200,000 people **reportedly** live in camps along the border between Sudan and the country of Chad. The nets protect refugees from mosquitoes. These insects spread malaria, which is a blood disease that can weaken or kill both children and adults who catch it.

To help raise money, Nothing but Nets held a sports camp for 250 young people in Chicago. The camp gave kids a **rare** opportunity to learn about basketball from Deng and other famous athletes. Deng gave campers **insight** into the threat of malaria in places where people sleep outside or in shelters without screens. One net covered with insect repellent costs only about $10. Yet it can last—and protect a person—for four years.

A SPECIAL AWARD In his short time in the NBA, Deng has impressed his fellow players. In 2007, NBA players voted Deng the Sportsman of the Year. This special award is for a player who sets a good example on and off the court. John Paxson, the general manager of the Chicago Bulls, spoke for many people when he said, "I think the world of [Luol Deng,] as a person and a player."

Deng's thank-you speech was short, sincere, and **believable.** "This award is on and off the court," he said. "It's something for me to give back to my parents. They will appreciate I'm being recognized for who I am."

WRAP IT UP

Find It on the Page

1. Why did Luol Deng and his family leave Sudan?

2. How do mosquito nets help people in Sudanese refugee camps?

3. Briefly summarize how Deng's life changed after he moved to the United States.

Use Clues

4. What do you think makes Deng want to help people in Sudan?

5. Suppose that someone asked you why it is important to help people in refugee camps. What would you say?

6. In your opinion, should other professional athletes use Deng as a role model? Why or why not?

Connect to the Big Question

After reading the article, do you think Deng's past helped make him the person he is today? Explain.

PROJECT: Interview

Answer the Big Question: What is the best way to find the truth?

You have read about issues that make people disagree. Now, use what you learned to answer the Unit 1 Big Question (BQ).

UNIT 1 ARTICLES

When Animals Help People, pp. 4–7

Learning the Truth in China, pp. 8–11

In the Grip of Graffiti, pp. 12–15

Cross Your Fingers! pp. 16–19

The Word on Bullies, pp. 20–23

Campers Give Peace a Chance, pp. 24–27

Return to Humanity, pp. 28–31

Luol Deng: A True Winner, pp. 32–35

STEP 1: Partner Up and Choose

Your first step is to pick Unit 1 articles that you like.

Get together. Find a partner to work with.

Read the list of articles. Discuss which articles listed on the left side of this page were the most interesting to you.

Choose two or more articles. Pick articles you both agree on.

STEP 2: Reread and Answer the Big Question

Next, answer the Unit BQ with your partner.

Reread the articles you chose. As you reread, think about the Unit BQ.

Interview your partner. For each article you chose, ask your partner these questions:

- What issue is this article about?
- What do the people in the article believe is true? How do they decide about the truth?
- How does the information in this article help you answer the Unit BQ: What is the best way to find the truth?

Take notes. As your partner answers the questions, take notes. Leave room for more notes you will take in the next steps.

STEP 3: Discuss and Give Reasons

Now, talk with your partner about his or her answer to the BQ.

Discuss your answers to the Unit BQ. Ask your partner to list reasons based on things he or she read in the articles:

- What details in the articles help you figure out the best way to find the truth? What do people think about when it comes to finding the truth?

Write your partner's answers. Add to your interview notes. Use another sheet of paper if you need to.

STEP 4: Add Examples

Now, finish the interview by asking for real-life examples.

Prompt your partner. Ask your partner about a time he or she had to decide what was true:

- Tell about a specific time you had to decide what was true. What problem did you face? How did you decide what was true?
- Do you think you made a good decision? Explain.

Add your partner's examples. Add to the interview notes. Be sure your notes have specific details.

STEP 5: Check and Fix

Next, you and your partner will look over the interview notes to see whether they could be improved.

Use the rubric. Use the rubric questions to evaluate your work. Answer each question yes or no. Then trade interview notes with your partner. Use the rubric to evaluate your partner's work, too.

Discuss your evaluations. Explain to your partner why you answered a question yes or no. For every no answer, explain what your partner could do to get a yes answer.

Improve your interview notes. If your interview notes could be improved, fix the mistakes or add more details.

STEP 6: Practice and Present

Get ready to present to your classmates.

Practice what you want to say. You will use your interview notes to explain how your partner answered the Unit BQ. Think about what you will need to say. Practice your presentation with your partner.

Present your interview notes. Introduce your partner to the class and explain how he or she answered the Unit 1 BQ. Include at least one specific example from an article and one from your partner's own experiences. Consider using a multimedia tool to summarize your main points for your audience.

RUBRIC

Do the interview notes . . .

- include an answer to the Unit BQ?
- have the titles of at least two articles from Unit 1?
- give at least one example from each article to explain the answer to the Unit BQ?
- give at least one specific real-life example to explain the answer to the Unit BQ?

Does every conflict have a winner?

Two teams played hard, but the game ended in a tie. Were there no winners, or was every player a winner? The articles in this unit describe conflicts in which there may or may not be a winner. One of these conflicts arises between people and wild animals who want to live in the same place. Think about the Big Question and who might be the winner in these conflicts—if there is a winner.

> Describe a game you played in, which you or your team did not technically win. Did you feel like a winner anyway? Why or why not?

Real-Life Connection

For many young people, athletes are role models. Kids not only look up to sports stars, kids want to be like them. However, not all athletes are good role models. On a diagram like the one below, list the names of athletes who you think are good influences on young people. Then list the names of athletes you think are bad influences. Are any athletes both good and bad? List their names in the middle of the diagram.

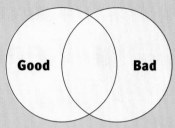

attitude (A tuh tood) *noun*   Your **attitude** toward something is the way you think or feel about it.
EXAMPLE: *Colin's positive **attitude** toward school shows in his perfect attendance record.*

competition (kahm puh TI shuhn) *noun*   A **competition** is a contest between individuals or teams.
EXAMPLE: *The championship game was a hard-fought **competition** between the two best teams in the league.*

disagreement (dis uh GREE muhnt) *noun*   A **disagreement** is a difference of opinion.
EXAMPLE: *My sister and I had a **disagreement** over whose turn it was to wash the dishes.*

prepare (pri PER) *verb*   When you **prepare,** you get ready to use or to do something.
EXAMPLE: *Last night, Yolanda read all her class notes to **prepare** for the test she had to take this morning.*

understanding (uhn duhr STAN ding) *noun*   An **understanding** is a knowledge of what something means.
EXAMPLE: *Now that Al has written several papers, he has a clear **understanding** of how to write good sentences.*

Does every conflict have a winner?

Do you have a jersey with your favorite sports star's name on it? You probably admire the athlete's sports skills. Do you also admire how your sports hero acts off the field? Some athletes set good examples, but others do not. As you read the article, ask yourself: **Should athletes be role models who help others "win"?**

Athletes as Role Models

▲ Dikembe Mutombo is a hero on and off the court.

The **competition** has been fierce. Only seconds are left in the game. A single point separates the two teams. The guard grabs the basketball and races down the court. He has only a split second to **prepare** his shot. He soars into the air and shoots. Suddenly, an enormous man raises his arm high above the basket. He grunts as he slams the shot back into the guard's face. Dikembe Mutombo, a giant at 7 feet 2 inches, has blocked another shot and saved a victory for his team.

For many years, Mutombo has saved games for his teams with his shot-blocking skills. However, Mutombo has also done something even more important off the court: He has helped save lives.

A MODEL FOR OTHERS Mutombo was born in the Democratic Republic of the Congo, in Africa. He came to the United States to study medicine. He planned to return to the Congo and be a doctor. However, he was soon recruited to play on the basketball team of the university he was attending. Later, he was recruited to play professional basketball. Once he did, he wanted to do more than make money. He wanted to help his homeland, too. Growing up in the Congo gave him a clear **understanding** of how hard life there can be. Mutombo wanted to put his money to good use to help other people.

In 1997, he started the Dikembe Mutombo Foundation. It buys medicine and medical equipment for people in the Congo. Thanks to Mutombo's work, a modern hospital will soon open there. When asked about the hospital, Mutombo said, "It gives a lesson to people who might be hesitant about contributing to the lives of others. This shows them that we can be part of the solution."

> Charles Barkley said, "I am not paid to be a role model. I am paid to wreak havoc on a basketball court."

SOSA SCANDAL Very few people would **disagree** that Mutombo is a good role model. Strong **disagreement** has arisen about other sports stars, however. One such star is baseball's Sammy Sosa.

In 2003, Sosa broke a bat grounding a ball to second base. When the umpire looked at a piece of the bat, he found that cork had been hidden inside. Some players believe that "corking" a bat helps them hit the ball farther. They think that the lighter a bat is, the easier it is to swing. Corking is against the rules of Major League Baseball (MLB). The umpire threw Sosa out of the game.

When Sosa was asked about the bat, he said that he ordinarily used it only for batting practice, "just to put on a show for the fans. I like to make people happy, and I do that in batting practice." He further explained that it was all a mistake. He did not mean to take the corked bat into the game.

To see whether Sosa had used a corked bat in other games, MLB had all the bats in Sosa's locker checked. They also tested bats that Sosa had used when he set records. None of the bats was corked. Was Sosa telling the truth about the corked bat? Was it all just a **misunderstanding?** Some disappointed fans say that it does not matter. Sosa should not have owned a corked bat in the first place.

BARKLEY BACK TALK Because of the Sosa controversy and others, many people began to question whether sports stars should be role models at all. The role-model question is not new. In an early ad in the 1990s, basketball star Charles Barkley said, "I am not paid to be a role model. I am paid to wreak havoc on a basketball court. Parents should be role models. Just because I can dunk a basketball, that doesn't mean I should raise your kids."

Though Barkley's **attitude** may not have been popular, he made a good point. Most people agree that parents should be kids' role models. No matter what anyone says, however, kids will continue to look up to athletes. Like it or not, athletes are role models for many young people. Stars like Dikembe Mutombo seem to **understand** this. He and other athletes like him set a good example for kids.

HUMANITARIAN HALL OF FAMERS The World Sports Humanitarian Hall of Fame has honored Mutombo for helping other people. The Hall, which encourages and rewards good role models in sports, has honored many other athletes. Here is a small sample of the men and women invited into the Hall:

- Kyle Petty (NASCAR)
- Drew Bledsoe (football)
- Mary Lou Retton (gymnastics)
- Johann Olav Koss (speed skating)
- Edgar Martinez (baseball)
- Babe Didrikson-Zaharias (golf)
- Andrea Jaeger (tennis)

WRAP IT UP

Find It on the Page

1. Who is Dikembe Mutombo and in what sport is he a star?

2. What has Dikembe Mutombo done to help people living in the Congo?

3. Briefly summarize the scandal mentioned in this article that involved Sammy Sosa.

Use Clues

4. Why do you think MLB has a rule against corked bats?

5. Do you think Charles Barkley was right when he said that parents should be kids' role models? Explain.

6. If you had to pick athletes to be in the Humanitarian Hall of Fame, how would you decide whom to honor?

Connect to the Big Question

After reading the article, do you think that athletes should be good role models for kids? Explain why or why not.

Real-Life Connection

How much do you know about coyotes? Rate your knowledge by checking the boxes on a chart like the one below.

Idea	Know a Lot	Know a Little	Know Nothing
What coyotes are			
Where coyotes usually live			
Where more and more coyotes live today			

Check It Out

The coyote (ky OH tee) is a member of the dog family. From a distance, the coyote looks a little like a German shepherd dog. Though coyotes and dogs are related, they are not friendly relatives. Coyotes are wild animals, and they will hunt and kill small dogs.

WORD BANK

conflict (KAHN flikt) *noun*   A **conflict** is an argument or a clash between opposing forces.
   EXAMPLE: *Every time I babysit my little brother, we have a **conflict** over his bedtime.*

danger (DAYN juhr) *noun*   When something is a **danger** to you, it is unsafe and could cause you harm.
   EXAMPLE: *The strong waves were a **danger** to the swimmers.*

outcome (OWT kuhm) *noun*   An **outcome** is a final result.
   EXAMPLE: *We were happy with the **outcome** of the game because we won by ten points.*

struggle (STRUH guhl) *verb*   When you **struggle** to do something, you find it hard to do yet keep on trying.
   EXAMPLE: *My dad and I had to **struggle** to push the car up the hill.*

Does every conflict have a winner?

Usually, people and wild animals stay out of each other's way. In recent years, however, land development has forced more wild animals to move closer to people. For example, coyotes have been spotted in people's yards. As you read the article, ask yourself: **Does anyone win when people and wild animals come into conflict?**

COYOTES ON THE GO

On a recent warm spring afternoon, diners in a Chicago sandwich shop had an unusual visitor. Through the open front door trotted a young coyote. He looked around, saw an open cooler full of bottled fruit juice, and without so much as a growl or a howl walked right in. As he lay down, amazed diners stood up. Though the cool coyote did not seem to be a **danger** to anyone, the diners and employees left the restaurant in fear. Some first grabbed their cell phones to snap photographs. It is not every day that a coyote wanders around a big city in broad daylight.

That might be changing, however. It seems that more coyotes have moved into city and suburban areas. Unfortunately, these wild new neighbors sometimes cause problems for the people who live there. People in the city and in the suburbs might find themselves in **conflict** with coyotes.

No one knows how many coyotes live in cities, but experts think that the number has grown. Why have coyotes traded in their homes on prairies for city life?

▲ Coyotes are so adaptable that they can live almost anywhere.

NO PLACE LIKE HOME To understand coyotes' situation today, you need to know about the past. American settlers cut down forests during the eighteenth and nineteenth centuries, creating more grassland. Settlers also began to kill off the coyote's natural enemy, the wolf. More prairies and fewer wolves meant more coyotes. By the twentieth century, coyote territory had grown from western North America to include nearly the entire continent.

Growth of Coyote Habitat

Before 1850
After 1850

Later in the twentieth century, the amount of open land coyotes lived on began to shrink. Cities grew, and suburbs were built on land that coyotes had once called home. However, unlike many wild animals, which **struggle** to survive when they lose their natural habitats (homes), coyotes did not become **endangered.** Instead of dying out, they moved out—into the city.

Coyotes can survive in the city because they are very adaptable. They can get used to life almost anywhere, even city life. Moreover, cities are not as hard for coyotes to live in as you might think. Paul Krausman, a biologist, explained to *National Wildlife* magazine: "In urban (city) areas, coyotes have got everything they need. There are no wolves or mountain lions, so they're at the top of the heap. People are throwing out garbage for them to eat, and they're watering their lawns, which attracts prey species. It's a perfect setup."

BEWARE OF THE COYOTE? Garbage may not sound like much of a meal to you, but coyotes do not mind eating it. They are not picky eaters. They do not believe in **struggling** to find food if they can help it. They will eat almost anything: small mammals, frogs, snakes, birds, and insects. If meat is not available, they will eat fruit or nuts. Unfortunately for pet owners, coyotes will also eat cats and small dogs. There are no statistics on the number of pets killed by coyotes. If the number of city coyotes increases, attacks on pets may increase.

Do the attacks make coyotes our enemies? If an enemy is someone or something that wants to harm us, then coyotes are not our enemies. The truth is that coyotes are usually not **dangerous** to people. That does not mean that you should try to get friendly with a coyote. The **outcome** would definitely *not* be in your favor. Coyotes have attacked people in California, Arizona, and other states.

Though coyote parents teach their pups to fear us, coyotes can lose their fear of humans if they come into contact with us often and without harm. Therefore, people who feed coyotes are asking for trouble. When coyotes get food from people, they connect the scent of humans with food, rather than with **danger.**

The safe thing to do is to keep your distance from coyotes. If you see a coyote nearby and it doesn't run away when it sees you, yell, wave your arms, and make yourself look as big as possible. Then wait for the coyote to run away.

To protect your pets from coyotes, follow a few simple rules. Do not leave your pets alone outside. Stand in a doorway or other safe place, and watch them. Do not feed your pets outdoors. Finally, put tight lids on outdoor garbage cans. To coyotes, open garbage cans are like fast-food restaurants. If your "restaurants" are closed, coyotes will go somewhere else to eat, and you and your pets will be safe.

WRAP IT UP

Find It on the Page

1. What is a coyote?
2. Why do coyotes find it fairly easy to live in the city?
3. Briefly summarize why coyotes have moved into cities and suburbs.

Use Clues

4. Why is it a bad idea for people to feed coyotes?

5. What advice would you give to neighbors who want to protect their pets from coyotes?
6. In your opinion, are coyotes enemies to people? Explain.

Connect to the Big Question

After reading the article, do you think coyotes are winners or losers in the struggle to find safe homes? Explain your opinion.

Real-Life Connection

Should the military treat soldiers who are parents differently from other soldiers? Find out what you think. Tell whether you agree or disagree with each statement below.

1. All people in the military should be treated the same.
2. Parents should not be allowed to serve in the military.
3. The military should pay for child care for soldiers' children.
4. If both parents in a family are soldiers, the military should not send them to war at the same time.

Check It Out

In the past, women could hold only certain jobs in the military, such as secretary or nurse. Today, more than 80 percent of military jobs are open to women. Women still cannot serve in units whose main mission is ground combat. However, they can hold other dangerous jobs, such as truck driver and fighter pilot.

desire (di ZYR) *noun* A **desire** is a strong wish or need.
EXAMPLE: *Macek's greatest **desire** is to be the starting quarterback for the school football team.*

opposition (ah puh ZI shuhn) *noun* If you feel **opposition** to something, you resist it or are against it.
EXAMPLE: *We were not able to change the school dress code because of our principal's strong **opposition** to the changes.*

plan (plan) *verb* When you **plan** something, you come up with a method or way to do it.
EXAMPLE: *Before I write a paper, I **plan** what I will say and how I will organize my ideas.*

resolution (re zuh LOO shuhn) *noun* A **resolution** is an ending to a problem or a conflict.
EXAMPLE: *When we could not agree on a movie, our mom's **resolution** of the problem was to rent three different movies.*

Does every conflict have a winner?

Today, the military sends far more female soldiers to war zones than it did in the past. Some people wonder whether it is right to send a woman who is also a mom to war—especially if her husband is a soldier in the same war. As you read the article, ask yourself: Do we need new laws to protect mothers and fathers in the military?

MOMS AND DADS IN THE MILITARY

Picture a young Marine fighter pilot married to a Navy lieutenant. He and his wife have two young daughters still at home. Not long ago, the couple faced a problem they did not **plan** for. The military ordered both of them to serve in the same war zone at the same time. Suddenly, the couple had to find someone else to take care of their children. Even worse, they had to think about what would happen if neither of them returned from the war. The wife summed up her feelings to a reporter: "It's a nightmare," she said.

Though the couple did not ask to serve together, some family members in the military do make that request. The most famous example is the five Sullivan brothers.

All five Sullivan brothers ▶ served on the same ship during World War II.

THE SULLIVAN BROTHERS During World War II, the brothers decided to join the U.S. Navy. Because they were close, they asked the navy to put them on the same ship. There was some **opposition** to the brothers' request. Navy leaders **opposed** the idea because they did not want five members of the same family lost at sea if their ship went down. Finally, however, the navy said yes because the brothers had such a strong **desire** to be together. The Sullivan case ended as the leaders' feared. In November 1942, enemy torpedoes sank the brothers' ship. The *Juneau* went down at sea, and all five of the Sullivan brothers lost their lives.

> As more women have joined the armed forces, it has become more common for husbands and wives to serve together.

After their deaths, the military changed its rules. A serviceman or servicewoman who is the only child left in a family may be removed from a war zone if two or more of the soldier's siblings were killed while serving in the navy, marine corps, or coast guard. There are no rules against a mother and father from the same family serving in the same war, however.

A NEW PROBLEM The truth is that the military did not expect this problem. Until recently, it was somewhat unusual for a husband and wife to serve together in the military. As more women have joined the armed forces, it has become more common for husbands and wives to serve together. A former navy lieutenant says, "It happens a lot more than we realize."

The lieutenant quoted above left the navy after discovering that she and her military husband could both be sent to war at the same time even if they had children. She strongly believes that a new law is needed to protect parents who serve in the military. Many other people agree that a new law is **desirable.** One California senator has tried to get Congress to pass a new law to protect military parents, but she has not yet succeeded.

Of course, not everyone agrees that a new law is needed. Some people believe that it would be unfair to treat military couples with children any differently from service people who are childless. Many military leaders are also against the idea of a new law. They think the problem of parents being sent to war at the same time does not happen often enough to make a new law necessary. Some people also argue that parents who sign up for the military make the sacrifice willingly. They are not forced into service. Therefore, they should also be willing to find ways to make sure their kids are cared for.

TO HELP No **resolution** to the problems of military parents is in sight. However, some groups have suggested ways that the military might help parents. For example, the National Women's Law Center has suggested that the military offer child-care services. Child care would help parents who have no one to turn to when they are called to war. Another, similar idea is to give military couples money for live-in babysitters. If both parents in a family are called to war, a sitter could watch the kids until other family members could take over.

In the meantime, the story of the fighter pilot and his lieutenant-wife has ended happily. She did not have to go to a war zone after all, because one of her daughters was less than one year old. Military rules say that a new mother can put off service until her baby is a year old. That was just one case, however. Other mothers and fathers can still be sent to war at the same time.

WRAP IT UP

Find It on the Page

1. Who were the Sullivan brothers?

2. How did the Sullivan brothers die during World War II?

3. What changes did the military make after the Sullivan case?

Use Clues

4. Why is the military against new laws for service people who are parents?

5. What do you think would happen if the military decided that parents could not be in the military?

6. In your opinion, should the military pay for child care? Explain.

Connect to the Big Question

After reading the article, what would you suggest doing to help military parents who are sent to war at the same time?

Real-Life Connection

Suppose you have a friend who plays a sport. Your friend's dad goes to every game and yells at referees, coaches—even at your friend sometimes. His behavior upsets your friend. In your opinion, what should your friend do? Write your thoughts in a chart like the one below.

I think my friend should . . .	I think this because . . .

WORD BANK

communication (kuh myoo nuh KAY shuhn) *noun*   **Communication** is the sharing of information or feelings.
EXAMPLE: *My mom and I have good **communication** because we have always talked over how we feel.*

competition (kahm puh TI shuhn) *noun*   A **competition** is a contest between individuals or teams.
EXAMPLE: *The **competition** to play on the soccer team was so fierce that Winona was proud the coach had chosen her.*

compromise (KAHM pruh myz) *noun*   When you reach a **compromise** with somebody, you both give up something you want in order to settle an argument.
EXAMPLE: *Dad wanted me home by nine P.M. rather than ten, but we reached a **compromise** by making my curfew nine-thirty.*

misunderstanding (mi suhn duhr STAN ding) *noun*   A **misunderstanding** is an incorrect idea of what someone else said or meant.
EXAMPLE: *Adrian thought I said to wear jeans to the dance, so I cleared up the **misunderstanding** by telling him to wear dress pants.*

perform (puhr FAWRM) *verb*   To **perform** is to do something or to use a special skill, such as dancing or acting.
EXAMPLE: *In science class, we are going to **perform** an experiment to see how water travels through the stems of plants.*

Does every conflict have a winner?

Have you ever seen adults yell at coaches or referees? Some adults who become too involved in kids' sports think that they are helping children succeed. Other people disagree. As you read the article, ask yourself: What happens when parents put too much pressure on kids to succeed in sports?

SPORTS PARENTS

Hall of Fame football coach Vince Lombardi once said, "Winning isn't everything; it's the only thing." Unfortunately, when it comes to kids' sports, many adults agree. Though sports **competition** should be fun, **competitive** adults sometimes ruin sports for kids. These adults believe that pushing young people to win is good for them. They say that children must learn how to **compete.** However, many experts disagree. They believe adults may **misunderstand** the effects of pushing young athletes too hard.

DISRUPTIVE DAD The father of tennis player Mary Pierce is a good example. Pierce was playing professional tennis by the time she was fourteen. Her father became so involved in her career that he quit his job to be her manager. "I've committed my whole life to my daughter," he told reporters.

▲ Young athletes can get a lot more out of sports than just the thrill of winning.

Though at first Pierce's father seemed supportive, his behavior soon became a problem. The only thing he cared about was that Mary win. He screamed at her during practice and after she lost. He shouted at her opponents. He even attacked a fan with whom he had had a **misunderstanding.** His behavior was so bad that the London newspaper the *Guardian* called him the "heavyweight champ of nightmare dads."

Pierce felt very uncomfortable when her father was at her matches. During one major tennis **competition,** he yelled so loudly and so often that he was asked to leave. Security guards walked him out of the stands and through the exit.

Finally, Pierce fired her father as her manager. In response, he sued her, saying that she owed him money. Father and daughter finally reached a **compromise.** She promised to pay him a large sum of money, and he promised to leave her alone. Now in her thirties, Pierce still plays professional tennis.

▲ **Mary Pierce figures out her next move during a tennis match.**

SPORTS BENEFITS Pierce's father and many adults like him do not seem to **understand** that there is more to sports than winning. Studies show that playing sports is good for both body and mind.

Playing sports is great exercise. It boosts the heart rate, strengthens muscles, and keeps people at a healthy weight. Equally important, sports exercise is good for the mind. When we exercise, the brain releases a chemical called beta-endorphin. This chemical can help us feel relaxed, happy, and full of energy.

Sports can also teach teamwork and the importance of clear **communication.** Teammates share the same goal—to play well—and must **communicate** with each other to achieve it. Sports can also teach young athletes how to **perform** well under pressure and to **compete** fairly with other people. Most important, playing sports is fun—or it should be. Having a good time is, in fact, the main reason that kids play sports. Adults should not lose sight of that fact.

HELPFUL DAD Of course, not all parents of athletes are overly **competitive.** Some parents manage to find a good balance between sportsmanship and competition. Take, for example, the father of baseball great Cal Ripken Jr. Cal Jr. gives his father credit for helping him succeed. He says that his dad introduced him and his brothers to baseball "in a way that got our interest and allowed us to go out there and **compete** and play. . . . Dad just had a nice even keel in the way that he approached baseball."

Cal Ripken Sr. and other parents like him show that adults can provide young athletes with the support that they need. That support is the right kind of adult involvement in kids' sports. It is the kind that helps young people do well in life as well as in sports. Adults should, after all, set good examples for kids.

WRAP IT UP

Find It on the Page

1. Who is Mary Pierce?

2. What are three health benefits of playing sports?

3. From the article, give an example of a sports parent who behaved badly and a sports parent who behaved well.

Use Clues

4. Why might it be hard for parents to not get involved when their children play sports?

5. Why do teammates need to communicate well?

6. Do you agree that fun is the main reason that kids play sports? Explain why or why not.

Connect to the Big Question

After reading the article, what do you think happens when parents put too much pressure on kids to succeed in sports?

Real–Life Connection

What do you know about kinship parenting? To find out, tell whether each statement below is true or false.

1. The only relative besides a parent who can become a child's legal guardian is a grandparent.
2. A kinship parent can become a permanent parent.
3. There are very few kinship parents in the United States.
4. A teenager cannot become a kinship parent.

Check It Out

Sometimes, an adult will volunteer to be a substitute parent when real parents cannot care for their children. If the substitute mother or father is the children's relative, or kin, the person is called a "kinship parent."

WORD BANK

assume (uh SOOM) *verb*   When you **assume** something, you suppose that it is true without checking to make sure.
EXAMPLE: *I was wrong to **assume** we had all the ingredients for the cake, because we were out of flour and sugar.*

challenge (CHA luhnj) *noun*   A **challenge** is something that is difficult and takes extra effort to do.
EXAMPLE: *Darnell said that running the twenty-six mile marathon was a true **challenge.***

desire (di ZYR) *noun*   A **desire** is a strong wish or need.
EXAMPLE: *After playing baseball all day in the hot sun, my only **desire** was to find a place to sit in the shade.*

obstacle (AHB sti kuhl) *noun*   An **obstacle** is something that blocks a path or keeps a person from doing something.
EXAMPLE: *Brenda's main **obstacle** to getting a summer job is that she does not have any work experience.*

understanding (uhn duhr STAN ding) *noun*   An **understanding** is a knowledge of what something means.
EXAMPLE: *Years of singing in a chorus have given Frannie a good **understanding** of how to read music.*

Does every conflict have a winner?

Grandparents are usually the first relatives to step in when parents cannot take care of their children. However, any relative who qualifies can become a kinship parent. As you read the article, ask yourself: When people make sacrifices to become kinship parents, do they win or lose?

THE KINDNESS OF KIN

The worried young woman stood in line with her three children. She had learned not to **assume** that the shelter would have room for her and her kids. She tried to count the number of people in front of her: one, two, three, four. . . . Minutes earlier, a worker had stood in the doorway and said that only a few beds remained. The woman was nervous. She had no **desire** to see her children sleep on the floor again.

The young woman had no job and almost no money. The children's father had left. Raising her children alone had become an almost impossible **challenge.** Finally, she decided to ask her aunt for help. She looked in her purse for coins to make the phone call.

Later, the aunt talked about the situation, "She told me she'd been put out on the streets, that she had nowhere to live. . . . She'd been in and out of shelters and didn't want her three kids to be living in places like that. She asked if I'd take them."

When parents cannot care for their kids, other family members may step in. This young man is parenting two young children.

The aunt agreed to care for the children until her niece had a job and a home. After she made this choice, however, the niece disappeared. The aunt thought about adopting the three children. However, she knew that her age—sixty—would be an **obstacle** to taking care of young children.

A HELPING HAND The aunt decided to see a social worker. He worked for the kinship care program at a nearby nursing school. The social worker found a summer day camp for the children. With the children in camp, the aunt had time to rest, think, and plan for her future with the children.

Kinship care programs give other kinds of help to people like the aunt. They tell kinship parents about sources of housing. They also help the parents find low-cost food and medical care. They work with the **understanding** that a person needs a helping hand to be a substitute parent because it is **challenging** to raise another person's children. For people who are up to the **challenge,** however, it can be a rewarding experience. Some experts believe it is often more **desirable** for kids to be raised by a family member than by someone whom they do not know.

In every state, children are living in families in which relatives are acting as their parents. For an idea of how many children are in kinship care, look at the chart.

SISTER AND MOM Many people **assume** that grandparents are always the kinship parents. However, the **assumption** that other family members are never kinship parents is untrue. For example, brothers and sisters have become kinship parents to younger siblings. One example of a sibling's becoming a kinship parent is the story of a young woman, Amy.

When Amy was a child, her mother did not take good care of Amy—or herself. Each time Amy's mother had another child, Amy stepped in to help. As her sister and three brothers grew older, they

CHILDREN IN KINSHIP CARE SELECTED STATES	
State	Number of Children
California	389,631
Minnesota	19,053
New York	165,493
Oklahoma	34,185
South Carolina	49,894
Texas	244,100
Vermont	1,838
Wyoming	2,738

Information is from the U.S. Census Bureau, Census 2000.

began to think of Amy as a second mother. Amy was often the one caring for the family. Amy was, in fact, a better parent than their real mom ever was.

One day, Amy told a social worker about the problems she faced at home. Amy and the other children were taken from their mother. They spent time in juvenile detention centers, foster care, and their grandmother's home. Life was not easy. It became worse, however, when Amy's mother was around. Finally, all the children were put into separate foster homes. By that time, Amy was a teenager with dreams of going to college and getting a degree.

When the children were together again, Amy promised to keep them together. She went to family court to ask about custody, and a judge named her legal guardian of her siblings for the next six months. Eventually, a judge would make Amy their foster parent.

In the end, Amy's **desire** to keep the kids together was even deeper than her **desire** to go to college. She worked two jobs to earn money to keep the kids and give them a comfortable home. It was a long battle, but Amy won. She overcame **obstacles** to become a permanent parent, and she says she is glad that she did.

WRAP IT UP

Find It on the Page

1. What is a kinship parent?

2. According to the article, how many children in California are in kinship care?

3. Briefly summarize how the young woman named Amy became a kinship parent.

Use Clues

4. What might be an advantage of having a relative care for kids who need parenting?

5. Where can kinship parents go to get help?

6. In your opinion, was the judge right to let someone as young as Amy become a kinship parent?

Connect to the Big Question

After reading the article, what do you think are some problems and rewards of being a kinship parent?

Real-Life Connection

What do you think this article will be about? Think about the title. Look over the article, and read the headings. Write the title and headings in a chart like the one below. In the below, write some notes on what you can tell about the article from previewing it.

Title:	Notes:
Headings:	

attitude (A tuh tood) *noun*   Your **attitude** toward something is the way you think or feel about it.
EXAMPLE: *Eduardo's classmates like to work with him because of his positive **attitude** toward schoolwork.*

conflict (KAHN flikt) *noun*   A **conflict** is an argument or a clash between opposing forces.
EXAMPLE: *To end the **conflict** over the referee's call, the game officials watched a recording of the play.*

obstacle (AHB sti kuhl) *noun*   An **obstacle** is something that blocks a path or keeps someone from doing something.
EXAMPLE: *Not knowing how to cook well is an **obstacle** to getting a job as a chef.*

opposition (ah puh ZI shuhn) *noun*   If you feel **opposition** to something, you resist it or are against it.
EXAMPLE: *To show his **opposition** to the student council's plan, Bill argued against it at the council meeting.*

style (styl) *noun*   A **style** is a particular way of doing something or expressing yourself.
EXAMPLE: *Kurt often plays his guitar in a blues **style**.*

Does every conflict have a winner?

It can be hard to compete against your own sister, especially when you are both tennis stars. Just ask Venus and Serena Williams. Off the court, they are good friends. On court, they are strong competitors. As you read the article, ask yourself: When siblings compete, does anyone win?

Sister Champions

V enus Williams was born in 1980. Her sister Serena was born in 1981. Their father, Richard, was a tennis coach. He began training both daughters to play tennis while they were still very young. He hoped that both of them would become stars. Before the girls were teenagers, they began to win tournaments and attract attention. However, Richard Williams made them stop playing in tournaments so that they could concentrate on school. Their mother, Oracene, had a strong **opposition** to putting sports above school.

Then, at age fourteen, Venus became a professional tennis player. Three years later, she surprised the world by reaching the final round of the U.S. Open, a major tennis competition. There, she ran into a serious **obstacle.** She had to play Martina Hingis, who was one of the best female tennis players in the world.

▲ Serena Williams (left) and her sister Venus proudly hold up tennis trophies they won.

Hingis beat Venus to win the championship. Nevertheless, Venus kept her confident **attitude,** and three years later she won the U.S. Open. At age eighteen, Venus was nearing the top of her game.

Serena Williams quickly followed in Venus's footsteps. She also became a pro at age fourteen. In fact, Serena was the first of the sisters to win one of the tennis world's most important tournaments, the U.S. Open. She defeated Martina Hingis to win in 1999. Since then, the Williams sisters have become two of the most famous tennis players in the world.

RAISED TO COMPETE—AND WIN Venus and Serena had played against each other as children. After 1999, they began having to compete against each other for some of the top prizes in tennis. Unlike matches they played when they were kids, these matches were on TV. Millions of people watched them play. Both sisters wanted to win championships. However, only one of them could win each time. How would sisters who had always been important in each other's life deal with these **conflicting** goals? People wondered whether someone could play well against his or her own sibling. Would their close relationship be an **obstacle** to success?

> Venus said, "I just hate to see Serena lose, even against me."

ONLY ONE CAN BE CHAMPION In October 1999, Serena defeated her sister for the first time. Later, the sisters played each other in a few tournaments. However, their most important match may have been in the U.S. Open in 2001. Venus defeated Serena and won her second U.S. Open championship in a row. Afterward, she said, "I don't exactly feel like I've won. If I was playing another **opponent,** I'd probably feel more joyful. I just hate to see Serena lose, even against me. I'm the big sister. I make sure she has everything, even if I don't have anything. I love her and it's hard."

Serena said, "I'm disappointed but only a little because Venus won. It was a bit tough out there. I was fighting the wind, fighting myself because I was making too many errors, and I was fighting Venus."

FAMILY OR SPORTS? The battles between Venus and Serena Williams on the tennis court led to victories for both sisters over the years. However, the competition has not changed either sister's **attitude** about the other. Moreover, their tennis rivalry has not led to **conflict** between them. They are close friends, and they encourage each other's career outside of tennis. Serena has taken her famous sense of **style** and started a business as a clothing designer. She also hopes to pursue a career in acting. Venus, also a clothing designer, has an interior design company.

The Williams sisters will probably be successful in whatever they choose to do. The most important thing for them, however, is being successful as members of a family. As Venus has said, "I think the best part about having a sister is that it's very inspiring. If I see her do well, or if I see her and she doesn't win a match, I'm always inspired and motivated by her, more than anyone else ever."

WRAP IT UP

Find It on the Page

1. Who are Venus and Serena Williams?

2. Why did Venus and Serena Williams stop playing competitive tennis when they were young?

3. What careers outside of tennis do Venus and Serena Williams have?

Use Clues

4. After winning the U.S. Open in 2001, why did Venus Williams say, "I don't exactly feel like I've won"?

5. If you had to compete against a close friend in an athletic event, what might you say to the friend first?

6. If you thought competing against a friend would hurt your friendship, what would you do to prevent harm?

Connect to the Big Question

After reading the article, what do you think people can learn about competition from Venus and Serena Williams?

Real-Life Connection

What do you know about zoos? Rate your knowledge on a chart like this one.

Idea	Know a Lot	Know a Little	Know Nothing
How zoos treat animals			
What endangered species are			
How zoos help endangered species			

Check It Out

Over 1,000 species, or kinds, of animals are now on the U.S. government's endangered species list. These animals are in danger of dying out and disappearing from the face of the earth. A law called the Endangered Species Act gives these animals special protection.

WORD BANK

challenge (CHA luhnj) *noun*   A **challenge** is something that is difficult and takes extra effort to do.
EXAMPLE: *My brother welcomed the **challenge** of being the first in our family to go to college.*

compromise (KAHM pruh myz) *noun*   When you reach a **compromise** with somebody, you both give up something you want in order to settle an argument.
EXAMPLE: *I wanted root beer, but my brother wanted ice cream, so we reached a **compromise** by making root beer floats.*

danger (DAYN juhr) *noun*   When something is a **danger** to you, it is unsafe and could cause you harm.
EXAMPLE: *The park district complained that the skateboarders were a **danger** to themselves and other people.*

disagreement (dis uh GREE muhnt) *noun*   A **disagreement** is a difference of opinion.
EXAMPLE: *We had a **disagreement** about whether we should watch a football game or a movie on television.*

outcome (OWT kuhm) *noun*   An **outcome** is a final result.
EXAMPLE: *The happy **outcome** of my dog's leg surgery is that he can run and jump again.*

Does every conflict have a winner?

Today, many zoo animals live in an environment that is similar to their natural homes. Still, many people believe that zoos are unfair to animals. As you read the article, ask yourself: **Should animals be put in zoos?**

Two Views of the Zoo

Not long ago, zoo animals lived in small cages. That way, the animals were not a **danger** to people who came to see them. It did not matter where an animal came from. Whether its home was warm and sunny or icy and gray, every zoo animal lived the same way. The sad **outcome** was that some animals had short, unhappy lives.

Zoos changed in 1972. That is the year a new kind of zoo opened in San Diego, California. The San Diego Wild Animal Park spread over 1,800 acres. The old-fashioned cages were gone. In their place, animals had large stretches of land to explore. There were still barriers to keep animals from running away. However, the barriers were hidden so people could not see them. The new zoo was a **compromise** between people's need for safety and animals' need for freedom. Zoos all over the world have also moved away from cages and have taken on the **challenge** of trying to give zoo animals a more natural place to live.

▲ A lion peers through the bars of the cage he lives in.

There is still **disagreement,** however, about whether zoos are good for the animals that live there. Some people believe that captivity, or keeping wild animals in zoos, is always wrong. These people say that sending animals to strange places is cruel. According to their studies, many zoo animals are unhappy in captivity. Are these people right?

IN PRAISE OF ZOOS People who are in favor of zoos say no. These people point out that zoos protect animals. They give **endangered** species safe homes and help keep the species alive. One way that zoos preserve species is through breeding programs. These programs help keep **endangered** species from dying out. For example, one species, the black-footed ferret, is no longer **endangered,** thanks to breeding programs in zoos.

This panda lives in a modern zoo.

People in favor of zoos also argue that zoos educate the public. These people believe that zoo education programs make the public want to take good care of animals. The more the public knows about animals, they argue, the more it will want to help them. They **disagree** with people who say that zoos are harmful.

AGAINST ZOOS Though breeding programs seem to help animals, some experts say the programs do not work. They point out that some species will not breed in zoos. Breeding giant pandas, for example, has been a serious **challenge.** People who are against zoos also say that zoos take more giant pandas from their natural habitat than are born through breeding programs.

Most people who are against zoos believe that animals, like people, have rights. One important right is the right to freedom. For example, the Australian animal rights group Animal Liberation complains that zoos do not respect animals' right to live naturally. The group says that zoo animals have "little opportunity to run, soar in the sky, swing through the trees, or roam over large distances."

Animal rights people believe that zoo animals are bored and unhappy. In the wild, they point out, animals spend much of their time hunting or looking for food. In a zoo, animals are fed every day and therefore have very little to do.

Finally, animal rights people say that we should try to visit animals in their natural habitats, not in zoos. If we cannot do that, they say, we can watch movies of animals. Moviemakers go into jungles and other settings to record how animals behave in the wild. Animal lovers can always watch the movies that result.

The debate about zoos goes on, with no end in sight. In the meantime, more than a thousand animal species remain on the **endangered** list. Whether you are for zoos or against them, keeping these animals alive for future generations is, perhaps, the most **challenging** problem of all.

WRAP IT UP

Find It on the Page

1. What is an endangered species?

2. How was the San Diego Wild Animal Park different from other, older zoos?

3. Briefly summarize the arguments in favor of zoos and the arguments against zoos.

Use Clues

4. What kinds of changes might animal rights groups like to see in zoos?

5. What do you think would happen if there were no zoos?

6. How would you answer someone who said there was nothing wrong with the way zoos used to be?

Connect to the Big Question

After reading the article, have your feelings about zoos changed? Explain why or why not.

Real-Life Connection

What do you think about age limits? To find out, tell whether you think each idea below is true or false.

1. People should have to retire at the age of sixty-five.
2. Young people should not be allowed to vote until they are eighteen years old.
3. Teens under the age of eighteen cannot be trusted with real responsibilities.
4. People older than sixty-five are no longer able to work at a real job.

Check It Out

The 26th Amendment lowered the voting age to eighteen. Today, there are movements in many states to lower the voting age again. On the other end of the timeline, the age at which workers can receive full retirement benefits from the government has been raised from sixty-five to sixty-seven.

WORD BANK

communication (kuh myoo nuh KAY shuhn) *noun*   **Communication** is the sharing of information or feelings.
EXAMPLE: *E-mail is a quick and easy form of **communication** between people.*

misunderstanding (mi suhn duhr STAN ding) *noun*   A **misunderstanding** is an incorrect idea of what someone else said or meant.
EXAMPLE: *I had a small **misunderstanding** with my classmate about when our project was due.*

resolution (re zuh LOO shuhn) *noun*   A **resolution** is an ending to a problem or a conflict.
EXAMPLE: *The **resolution** of my money problem was simple: spend less and save more.*

struggle (STRUH guhl) *verb*   When you **struggle** to do something, you find it hard to do yet keep on trying.
EXAMPLE: *I was so tired this morning that I had to **struggle** to get up and get dressed.*

subject (SUHB jikt) *noun*   A **subject** is a topic or focus of discussion.
EXAMPLE: *I have not chosen a **subject** for my essay, but I might write about changes in voting laws.*

Does every conflict have a winner?

Do we need laws to say that you cannot vote until you are a certain age? Do we need laws to say that you have to retire at a certain age? As you read the article, ask yourself: Is there a "right age" to start voting or stop working?

Either Too Young or Too Old

Age limits are once again the **subject** of debate. United States law says people cannot vote until they are eighteen. The law also discourages people from retiring until they are sixty-seven. Should we be making important decisions about people based on their age? Americans are divided on this issue.

TOO YOUNG TO VOTE The voting age is one area of controversy. Some teenagers and adults want to lower the voting age to sixteen. However, many people are against the idea. These people argue that teenagers have not had enough experience to make good decisions. They also argue that teens do not know enough about government to vote. One group that disagrees is the National Youth Rights Association (NYRA). The NYRA thinks that sixteen-year-olds should be able to vote. Group members have **communicated** facts and statistics to the press to support this view. The group's findings may come as a surprise to you.

According to the NYRA, sixteen-year-olds who take part in We the People, an educational program about the Constitution, are qualified to vote.

An older woman helps young people register to vote.

QUALIFIED TO VOTE To prove it, the NYRA cites a survey in which a group of sixteen-year-olds who took the program answered a list of questions. A group of adults aged eighteen to eighty were asked the same questions. The sixteen-year-olds answered more questions correctly than the adults did.

For example, 96 percent of the sixteen-year-olds surveyed knew the name of the vice president of the United States. Only 74 percent of adults surveyed could name the vice president. Also, 96 percent of students surveyed knew the meaning of the term *judicial review*. Judicial review is the power of a court to judge whether laws are in keeping with the Constitution. Only 66 percent of adults surveyed could explain the term.

One New York City Council member uses different arguments to support the view that sixteen-year-olds should be allowed to vote. She believes that teens who have adult responsibilities should also have the adult right to vote. She says, "A thirteen-year-old can be tried as an adult. A sixteen-year-old can drive and have a job. Teens need to have a say in the policies and decisions that affect their lives."

> **Teens need to have a say in the policies and decisions that affect their lives.**

No matter which side of this issue you are on, it is hard to doubt this: People do not magically change on their eighteenth birthday. They are much the same as they were the day before. The same is true of older people who have birthdays and are nearing retirement.

WORKING AFTER SEVENTY Traditionally, most people in the United States retired at age sixty-five. In a 2005 poll, however, almost three fourths of workers surveyed say that they plan to keep working past the traditional retirement age.

There are many reasons that people choose to keep working. Some people are afraid that life without work will be boring. Other people cannot afford to retire. They have not saved a lot of money, and if they no longer worked, they would have to **struggle** to pay their bills.

Unfortunately, some older people who want to keep working may face problems at work. Many companies still expect every employee to retire by the age of sixty-seven. Some employers believe that older workers are unable to do a good job. Also, companies as a whole have not planned for a large number of older workers to stay on the job. Moreover, **communication** between companies and older workers is not always good, which can lead to **misunderstandings.**

One **resolution** of the problem of forced retirement is part-time work. Staffing experts say that more and more people are trying a combination of retirement and work. For instance, some older people work three days a week, for 60 percent of their original pay. They might also take part of the pension, or retirement pay, that they would have gotten had they retired completely.

Still, at many workplaces, employees can either earn a salary or collect a retirement pension. They cannot do both. These kinds of rules may add to the problems of **struggling** older Americans.

It may just be that both younger and older groups are victims of a **misunderstanding** about the importance of age. There are many bright, mature teenagers around. There are also many strong, active older people. Maybe both young and old would gain from being judged by who they are rather than how old they are.

WRAP IT UP

Find It on the Page

1. How old does a U.S. citizen have to be in order to vote?

2. List three arguments in favor of lowering the voting age.

3. Briefly summarize why some people work past age sixty-five.

Use Clues

4. Why might sixteen-year-old students find it easier than adults to answer questions about U.S. government?

5. What kinds of knowledge do you think people should have in order to vote?

6. If you could vote at age sixteen, would you? Explain.

Connect to the Big Question

After reading this article, do you think there is a "right age" to vote or to retire? Explain.

 **Debate**

 Answer the Big Question: Does every conflict have a winner?

You have read about different conflicts. Now, use what you learned to answer the Unit 2 Big Question (BQ).

UNIT 2 ARTICLES

Athletes as Role Models,
pp. 40–43

Coyotes on the Go,
pp. 44–47

Moms and Dads in the Military,
pp. 48–51

Sports Parents,
pp. 52–55

The Kindness of Kin,
pp. 56–59

Sister Champions,
pp. 60–63

Two Views of the Zoo,
pp. 64–67

Either Too Young or Too Old,
pp. 68–71

STEP 1: Form a Group and Choose

Your first step is to pick Unit 2 articles that you like.

Get together. Find a small group to work with.

Read the list of articles. Discuss which articles listed on the left side of this page were the most interesting to you.

Choose two or more articles. Pick articles that you all agree on.

STEP 2: Reread and Answer the Unit Big Question

Your next step is to begin forming your viewpoint for a debate.

Reread the articles you chose. As you reread, think about the Unit BQ.

Answer questions. For each article you chose, answer these questions:

- What conflict is the article about?
- Does anyone in this conflict win? Does anyone lose?
- How would you answer the Unit BQ: Does every conflict have a winner?

Form groups for the debate. Divide your small group into two opposing teams. One team will present the viewpoint *Yes, every conflict has a winner.* The other team will present *No, every conflict does not have a winner.*

STEP 3: Find Examples and Discuss Reasons

During this step, begin to develop your argument.

Find examples in the articles. Support your answer to the Unit BQ by using examples of conflict from the articles you chose. Your examples should clearly support the idea that every conflict does or does not have a winner. List examples that support your position.

Discuss your reasons. With your team, choose the most convincing reasons. Underline them to use in the debate.

STEP 4: Strengthen Your Argument

Now, finish your debate argument.

Choose the examples for your argument. Look over the examples and discuss which ones best support your argument. Underline the ones that are most convincing.

Discuss how to present your argument. Consider these points as you prepare your presentation:

- Think about your audience. Which reasons do you think they will find the most convincing?
- Put your reasons in order. Start with the least convincing reason and end with the most convincing one. Doing this will leave a strong impression with your audience.

STEP 5: Strengthen Your Work

Next, you and your team will discuss your debating points to be sure that you have a convincing argument.

Use the rubric. Use the questions to evaluate your work. Answer each question yes or no.

Discuss your evaluations. If you have yes answers, can you make those debating points even stronger? If you have any no answers, what can you do to change your argument before you present it?

Improve your argument. Look over your reasons again to be sure that you have chosen convincing ones. Improve your argument before you present it to your class.

STEP 6: Practice and Present

Get ready to debate.

Practice what you want to say. Divide the debating points among your group members. Be sure you have your reasons in order from least to most convincing. You want to end on a strong note.

Present your viewpoint. Present your side of the debate, and the other team will present theirs. You might take turns with the other team—each member of each team presenting a reason and examples to support it. Which reasons do classmates think were most convincing? Why?

What should we learn?

If you want to ride a bike, it might be a good idea to learn how to fix it before you ride. What else is important to learn? The articles in this unit explore different ideas about learning. What can you learn from dreams? What can you learn to conquer your fears? As you read, think about what people should learn. You may learn a few new ideas yourself.

Think about one of the most important things you have ever learned. What did you learn? How did you learn it? Why was it so important to know?

Real-Life Connection

Someday within your lifetime, people may travel to Mars. How much do you know about Mars? Rate your knowledge on a chart like the one below.

Idea	Know a Lot	Know a Little	Know Nothing
Where Mars is			
What Mars is like			
Whether people could live there			

Check It Out

Mars is the fourth planet from the sun. Earth is the third. When Mars is closest to Earth, it is still about 34 million miles away.

WORD BANK

discover (dis KUH vuhr) *verb*   When you **discover** something, you find it or learn about it for the first time.
EXAMPLE: *Jennifer was happy to **discover** her favorite wool scarf at the back of the hall closet.*

explore (ik SPLAWR) *verb*   When you **explore** a place, you look it over carefully to learn more about it.
EXAMPLE: *Austin likes to **explore** the beach near his dad's house.*

facts (fakts) *noun*   **Facts** are pieces of information that can be shown to be true.
EXAMPLE: *To get a library card, Emilio had to give several **facts** about himself, including his age, address, and telephone number.*

organize (AWR guh nyz) *verb*   When you **organize** something, you use a system to put it in order.
EXAMPLE: *To **organize** the ideas in my story, I will tell what happened first, next, and last.*

possible (PAH suh buhl) *adjective*   When something is **possible,** it can be done or can happen.
EXAMPLE: *My dance teacher said that if I practice every day, it might be **possible** for me to win the dance contest.*

What should we learn?

Many scientists believe that people will be able to live on Mars someday. That day may come sooner than you think. As you read the article, ask yourself: What do we need to learn about Mars to live there?

Travel to Mars

Imagine this ad popping up on your computer screen: "Have the vacation of a lifetime! Let us **organize** a trip to our neighbor planet, Mars, for you. **Explore** the natural wonders of the best little planet in the solar system. Visit Happy Face Crater, and **discover** just how interesting a crater can be. See Olympus Mons, the biggest volcano in the solar system. Grab a friend and dance in the light of not one moon, but two!"

Of course, you should not start packing just yet. Right now, it is not **possible** to take a vacation on Mars. Before you can do that, some difficult problems have to be solved.

ONE-WAY TICKET? The first problem is distance. The cold, hard **facts** are that Mars is at least 33.9 million miles away, so it takes a lot of fuel to get there. Transport would be difficult. Even at a speed of 18,000 miles an hour, the highest speed at which spaceships go today, the trip would take months. Moreover, the trip might be one-way. It takes so much fuel to go to Mars that the ship might not have room for fuel to return home.

▲ **This picture of Mars, taken by one of the Viking orbiters, shows some of the craters on the planet.**

The distance does not make travel to Mars **impossible.** Though scientists cannot bring Mars closer to Earth, they can try new power sources, which might make the distance seem shorter. One **possibility** is nuclear energy. National Aeronautics and Space Administration (NASA) officials say it might be **possible** to use a small nuclear reactor to produce energy on the ship. That way, the ship would have an almost unlimited power supply. It could travel faster, too. In **fact,** the trip to Mars might take only two months.

BUNDLE UP AND BRING OXYGEN Getting to Mars is one thing. Living there is another. Mars is so cold that you could freeze to death quickly there. The average temperature near the ground is 60 degrees below zero. It would feel colder than that, however, because Mars is also windy. Winds can blow at speeds up to 80 miles an hour.

Worse yet, it would be **impossible** to breathe without help. Less than 1 percent of the air on Mars is oxygen. To live there, you would have to bring—or make—oxygen for yourself.

Even if you had enough oxygen, you would probably get sick. Scientists have **discovered** that living in outer space for a long time can change the human body. Cosmic rays—high-speed particles zipping around the galaxy—could harm your cells. In addition, living in a weightless environment for so long could cause your heart, muscles, and bones to grow weak.

Special clothes, light oxygen tanks, and good exercise routines are just some of the possible solutions to these problems. Inflatable shelters—rubber or plastic homes that have walls filled with air—might solve some of the weather and health problems for people trying to live on Mars.

PACK A BIG LUNCH That leaves just a few more big problems—namely, getting food and water. **Exploration** of Mars has shown there are no plants or animals there. That means there is nothing to eat. Mars does have a small amount of groundwater, but it is frozen solid. Long ago, there was probably water on the surface of Mars, but it is gone.

THE AIR ON MARS

argon 1.6% oxygen .13%

nitrogen 2.7%

carbon dioxide 95%

Information is from "Mars Facts," http://athena.cornell.edu/mars_facts.

If you happen to be planning a Mars vacation well ahead of time, relax. The food and water problems could possibly be solved before long. To get water, for example, people might melt the ice that is on Mars. The water could then be recycled to grow grain and vegetables inside shelters. Though finding food on Mars would not be as easy as going to the supermarket, with these special gardens for fruits and vegetables it would no longer be the problem it is today. On the other hand, you might want to pack a chicken or two. Mars probably will not be ready for livestock for quite a while.

One small problem remains: getting along with other travelers. The first people to go to Mars and build a settlement will spend a lot of time together. Scientist Richard Berendzen puts it this way: "Five or six of your closest friends in a room the size of your living room for three years—that's a tough thing to do." One thing on Mars is not a problem: time. A Martian day is about 40 minutes longer than an Earth day. A Martian year is almost twice as long as an Earth year. That is a long time to wait for a birthday.

WRAP IT UP

Find It on the Page

1. About how long would it take to get to Mars with today's fuels?

2. What kind of fuel might shorten the trip to only a few months?

3. List three problems that have to be solved before people can live on Mars.

Use Clues

4. Why might scientists be so interested in exploring Mars?

5. What advice would you give to people getting ready to travel to Mars?

6. If you had a chance to travel to Mars, would you take it? Explain.

Connect to the Big Question

Now that you have read the article, what do you think we need to learn before people can live on Mars?

Real-Life Connection

Some people think there are differences between the way boys speak and the way girls speak. Do you agree? See what you think. For each pair of statements below, tell which statement you think was made by a boy and which was made by a girl.

Pair 1
- "You are completely wrong."
- "You might want to rethink that point a little."

Pair 2
- "I can see you are having a pretty hard time with this."
- "Listen to me, because I know just how to fix your problem."

Pair 3
- "That is easy! I know the answer."
- "Excuse me, but I think I might know."

WORD BANK

analyze (A nuh lyz) *verb*   When you **analyze** something, you divide it into parts and see how they fit together.
    EXAMPLE: *To help me **analyze** how an engine works, my dad took one apart and then helped me put it back together again.*

investigate (in VES tuh gayt) *verb*   When you **investigate** something, you find information about it in order to understand it better.
    EXAMPLE: *I decided to **investigate** why my dog was barking.*

question (KWES chuhn) *verb*   When you **question** something, you challenge the truth of it.
    EXAMPLE: *Though Ed did not agree with Tori, he did not **question** her opinion, because he knew she had given it a lot of thought.*

topic (TAH pik) *noun*   A **topic** is a subject or general idea.
    EXAMPLE: *Oksana loves to play basketball, so she chose the sport as the **topic** of her report.*

understand (uhn duhr STAND) *verb*   To **understand** is to know the meaning of something.
    EXAMPLE: *After we did a few story problems together in math class, I began to **understand** how to solve them.*

What should we learn?

Sometimes, boys and girls have trouble understanding one another. Is that because males and females have different ways of communicating? As you read the article, ask yourself: **What can we learn from differences in speaking styles?**

Look Who's Talking

Look at the people around you in class. Think back to what they recently said, and **analyze** it. Did the boys use words and sentences different from those the girls used? Did the boys speak more confidently than the girls did?

Some people would probably answer yes to both questions. They believe that males and females have different speech styles, or ways of speaking. They also think that the differences can make it hard for boys and girls to **understand** one another.

To test these ideas, language experts have worked to **investigate** the ways that males and females speak. After **analyzing** many conversations, some experts say they hear definite differences in the speech styles of males and females.

WHAT'S THE DIFFERENCE? One difference lies in the **topic** of conversation. Some language experts believe that boys talk most often about things, while girls tend to talk most often about feelings.

▲ The speech style of the boys in this picture may be different from that of the girls.

For instance, boys might chat about cars, sports, and games. Girls, on the other hand, might talk about what is happening in their friends' lives.

Language experts also believe that a boy tends to speak to show that he is the top person in a group. When a girl speaks, she tends to mean for her words to make people feel equal and comfortable. Language expert Deborah Tannen sums up the difference this way: "From childhood, girls criticize peers who try to stand out or appear better than others." In contrast, males, she says, "learn to use talking as a way to get and keep attention."

Finally, the language experts believe that boys often sound more confident than girls. They say that boys are more likely to give orders and to insist that they are right. In contrast, girls are more likely to say they do not **understand** something. As a result, girls more often say "maybe" or "I guess" to be polite. Boys, on the other hand, more often interrupt other people and may speak more loudly than girls.

ARE THEY RIGHT? Not everyone agrees that there are male and female speaking styles. Some people who **question** this theory say that it is impossible to tell whether a statement is "male" or "female." Suppose someone says, "I think that is a great idea!" If you do not know who made the statement, you might think that a boy said it, because it is bold and confident. On the other hand, you might think that a girl said it, because it shows support for someone else.

Here is another problem with the boy-girl theory of language. What if you knew it was a boy who said, "I think that is a great idea!" Because you knew it was a boy, would you think that the statement was bold and confident? Now, imagine you knew that the speaker was a girl. Would you think that the statement was friendly?

A DIFFERENT OPINION Language expert Deborah Cameron has **questioned** the theory that males and females have different speaking styles and pointed out many problems with it. Consider how males and females might turn down a request for a favor. You may expect boys to be direct and just say no. You might expect girls to try to be courteous. However, Cameron believes that both boys and girls make an effort to be polite. She thinks that most people, male or female, try not to hurt others' feelings when saying no.

Cameron's **investigations** into this theory also found that boys do not interrupt conversations much more than girls interrupt conversations. She believes that a careful look at language studies shows that boys and girls interrupted one another about the same number of times.

In short, Cameron believes that the speaking-style theory is just plain wrong. She thinks that we expect males and females to speak differently, and if we expect to find something, we usually find it.

Which group of experts is right? You decide. Listen closely to the way your classmates speak to one another. See if you hear a difference between the ways boys and girls speak. Be **analytical.** Also be careful, though. You might just hear what you expect to hear.

WRAP IT UP

Find It on the Page

1. According to speaking-style theory, how are "boy topics" different from "girl topics"?

2. What difference does Deborah Tannen see between "girl talk" and "boy talk"?

3. Briefly summarize Deborah Cameron's ideas about speaking styles.

Use Clues

4. What problems might be caused by differences in speaking styles?

5. How might you test the speaking-style theory to see whether it is correct?

6. Which theory of speaking-style do you think is correct? Explain.

Connect to the Big Question

Now that you have read the article, what do you think we can learn from differences in speaking styles?

Real-Life Connection

What do you know about Native Americans? To help you find out, write whether each statement below is true or false.

1. Native Americans were the first Americans.
2. There are very few Native Americans left in the United States.
3. Most Native Americans live on reservations.
4. All Native Americans have the same traditions.

Check It Out

Native Americans are sometimes called "First People" because they were the first people to live in the Americas. European explorer Christopher Columbus called Native Americans "Indians" because he thought he had reached the islands in Southeast Asia known as the Indies.

WORD BANK

evaluate (i VAL yuh wayt) *verb*   When you **evaluate** someone or something, you form an opinion based on what you know.
EXAMPLE: *After I play a game, I think about what I did and try to **evaluate** how well I played.*

inquire (in KWYR) *verb*   When you **inquire** about something, you ask questions about it.
EXAMPLE: *Sean went to the store to **inquire** about a job.*

interview (IN tuhr vyoo) *noun*   In an **interview,** a person asks another person a series of questions.
EXAMPLE: *The sports reporter planned to ask many difficult questions at her **interview** with the coach.*

knowledge (NAH lij) *noun*   **Knowledge** refers to all of the information and ideas that you have learned.
EXAMPLE: *Kelly has a lot of **knowledge** about computers because she and her mom built one.*

What should we learn?

The people of the United States come from many cultures. Because the traditions of these cultures are different, misunderstandings sometimes result. People sometimes hurt each other without meaning to. As you read the article, ask yourself: Why is it important to learn about cultures different from your own?

MAKING SPORT OF TRADITION

Have you ever hurt someone's feelings without **knowledge** of doing so? Maybe you said or did something hurtful without meaning to. That is the case with some schools and cities that have named their sports teams after Native Americans.

There are many such teams. In fact, more than 3,000 sports teams in the United States have names like Chiefs, Indians, and Braves. Some teams have mascots dressed as Native Americans—or dressed as some people imagine Native Americans to dress. Are these names and mascots unkind to Native Americans? Are they racist?

ACCIDENTALLY UNKIND Many people say the names and mascots *are* racist. These people want teams to respect Native American culture. They **inquire** about how other groups would feel if teams were named after them.

▲ **This young man is dressed in the traditional clothing worn by fancy dancers in his tribe.**

For example, would African Americans, Mexican Americans, or Jewish Americans like it if teams took their names?

Those who want to keep the team names reply that the names honor Native Americans. They say that the names are meant to be fun, not disrespectful. In addition, they point out that there are sports teams named after other ethnic groups. The Notre Dame Fighting Irish and the Boston Celtics are two examples.

▲ In some places, Native Americans and other people disagree about how land should be used.

NATIVE AMERICAN REPLY People who are against the names and mascots believe that these things make fun of Native American culture and **values.** An Oneida woman explained, "We see objects sacred to us—such as the drum, eagle feathers, face painting, and traditional dress—being used, not in sacred ceremony, or in any cultural setting, but in another culture's game." In short, she and many other Native Americans are upset that their religious symbols are used to celebrate sporting events. They are also unhappy that the mascots make it seem as if all Native American groups are alike. In reality, different groups have different traditions.

Those who oppose the mascots also argue that the mascots make it seem as if Native American culture is dead. These people point out that more than 4 million Americans identify themselves as Native American or part Native American. Many of these Americans keep Native American traditions even if they do not live on reservations.

SACRED GROUND Team names and mascots are not the only things that some Native Americans find disrespectful. In recent years, Native Americans have tried to stop people from building in places where Native Americans are **known** to have been buried long ago. For example, builders in California found more than 400 remains of the Tongva people. Scientists came to move the bones. However, some

Native Americans do not want the remains to be moved. They believe that their burial grounds are sacred and should be left untouched. They fight to protect the land against development.

Land developers argue that too much money would be lost if they stopped building. The developer who unearthed the Tongva burial grounds also said that if anything was moved to preserve the burial grounds, workers might unearth even more remains. The developer fears he would be sued if that happened.

Many Native Americans **evaluate** the situation differently. They say that honoring the dead is far more important than making money. "I cried for 45 minutes," said one Tongva man who saw a crushed skull at a building site.

Similar clashes happen in many parts of America. Some are over burial grounds; others are over the loss of important relics. In one **interview,** a chief said, "When an Indian is buried, he's buried. You're not supposed to dig him up again." A Dakota leader believes digging up graves disturbs the spirits. He said, "Our belief is that nothing or no one ever dies; we just turn into something else and live on."

WRAP IT UP

Find It on the Page

1. What is a mascot?

2. About how many Americans identify themselves as full or part Native American?

3. Briefly summarize the arguments of people who oppose teams' use of Native American names and mascots.

Use Clues

4. What is the Native Americans' disagreement with land developers based on?

5. How do you think the problems between Native Americans and other Americans might be solved?

6. Who do you think is right—the land developers or the Native Americans who are against them? Explain.

Connect to the Big Question

Now that you have read the article, tell whether you think it is important to learn about other people's cultures and why.

Real-Life Connection

Imagine this situation. It is the night before a big, important test. You have studied, but you may not have studied enough. That night, you dream about taking the test. In your dream, you find it easy to answer all the questions, and you are confident that you answered them all correctly. Because you dreamed you would do well, would you feel more confident about doing well on the day of the test than you would have felt otherwise? Why or why not?

Check It Out

Everyone dreams, except for a few people who have had brain injuries or illnesses. If you think you do not dream, you probably do not remember your dreams. Most dreams happen during a type of sleep called rapid-eye movement, or REM. Adults spend about 20 to 25 percent of sleep time in REM sleep. During that type of sleep, your closed eyes flutter.

WORD BANK

curiosity (kyoor ee AH suh tee) *noun*   When you have **curiosity** about something, you have an interest in learning about it.
EXAMPLE: *From the way our new kitten runs around the apartment, I would say she has **curiosity** about everything!*

examine (ig ZA muhn) *verb*   When you **examine** something, you look at it very carefully.
EXAMPLE: *The doctor told Janelle that he would need to **examine** her ankle to see whether it was broken.*

information (in fuhr MAY shuhn) *noun*   If you have **information** about something, you know the facts about it.
EXAMPLE: *Do you have any **information** about when our research report is due?*

recall (ri KAWL) *verb*   To **recall** something is to remember it.
EXAMPLE: *Steve used the new words as often as he could so that he could **recall** what they meant.*

What should we learn?

For centuries, people have tried to figure out what their dreams mean. After all that time, though, we are still not sure why we dream or whether our dreams have meaning. As you read the article, ask yourself: **What can we learn from our dreams?**

In Your Dreams

You are walking down a city street. Everything is black-and-white. You turn a corner, and suddenly the world is colored. Down an alley, you see a purple cat with green stripes. When you approach it, it faces you and starts reciting your favorite rap. "I must be dreaming," you tell yourself.

Can you **recall** having a strange dream like that? Why are dreams filled with so many weird events? Doctors who study sleep and dreams might have an answer. They say that when you dream, your emotions and memories are active. However, the wide-awake, sensible side of your thinking is not. As a result, your dreams may seem like fantasy movies or cartoons. Dr. Patricia Garfield explains that we are "poets in our brain; we're creating images out of emotions." She says dreams are "picture thinking."

THE MYSTERIOUS WHY Does this "picture thinking" mean anything? People have long had **curiosity** about their dreams. To this day, however, no one is certain why we dream.

▲

When the wide-awake, sensible part of the brain shuts down, the imagination can take over.

Over the centuries, people have had many different theories about dreams. In ancient times, people took dreams very seriously. These people thought that dreams were messages from the gods, and they believed that dreams could inform them about the future. To get **information** about a dream's meaning, a person might go to a soothsayer—someone who was believed to be able to tell the future—to discover what the dream meant.

FEARS OR UNWANTED FILES? Today, we have very different ideas about what, if anything, dreams mean. Some experts believe that dreams show us sides of ourselves we hide when we are awake. Dreams may also show us our deepest wishes and fears.

Take, for example, the strange dream a teacher had. It happened the night before she began a break from school to have a baby. That night, she dreamed that she was in a speeding car. In her dream, she was terrified. She screamed, "Slow down! Slow down!" As she looked more carefully at the driver, she saw it was the substitute who was taking over her classes. The teacher was afraid the substitute would try to teach difficult **information** too quickly. Her dream about the speeding car expressed that fear.

The teacher's dream is an example of the way dreams may reveal deep feelings. Not everyone thinks that dreams work that way, however. Some experts think that dreaming is nothing more than a nightly cleanup of the brain. According to them, the brain throws out junk memories—**information** not worth **recalling.** Just as we clear our computers of unneeded files, our brains get rid of memories we do not need.

Common Symbols in Dreams	
Symbol	Possible Meaning
car	freedom, escape
dancing	freedom, love
fog	confusion, fear
mountain	difficult goal

ANALYZE THIS! If you are **curious** about what, if anything, a dream of yours means, try to **recall** the dream clearly. Jot down everything that you can remember. Then **examine** your dream the same way you might **examine** a poem or a story. One aspect to consider is symbols. A symbol is something that stands for something else. For example, a rose can be a symbol of love, and a flag can be a symbol of a country.

The idea that dreams contain symbols is a theory, not a fact. However, it is a theory that many people believe. A symbol might represent the same thing to most people. However, it might also mean different things to different people. For example, a bicycle might represent travel to one person, childhood to another person, and loss of balance to a third person.

For each picture that might be a symbol, ask yourself what words and ideas the picture brings to mind. For instance, the picture of a bicycle might make you think of words like *wheel, steer, fall,* and *travel.* Ask yourself which, if any, of these words connect with something important that is going on in your life right now.

In the end, the meaning of a dream is a matter of opinion. No one can say for sure whether your opinion about a dream is wrong or right. You might dream about an air conditioner and think it represents how cool you are—and you just might be right!

WRAP IT UP

Find It on the Page

1. According to Dr. Garfield, why are dreams sometimes filled with strange events?

2. In ancient times, what did people think dreams were?

3. Briefly summarize a modern theory about dreams.

Use Clues

4. What example can you find in the article of a dream that shows a person's fears?

5. Why might people be so curious about dreams?

6. In your opinion, do dreams mean anything? Explain your answer.

Connect to the Big Question

Now that you have read the article, what do you think we can learn from our dreams?

Real-Life Connection

What do you think of when you hear the word *teamwork*? Jot down your ideas in a word web like the one below.

Teamwork

help each other

WORD BANK

analyze (A nuh lyz) *verb*   When you **analyze** something, you divide it into parts and see how they fit together.
EXAMPLE: *Max and I started to **analyze** the movie by summarizing what happened in the beginning, middle, and end.*

background (BAK rownd) *noun*   Your **background** is made up of your experiences, knowledge, and education.
EXAMPLE: *Jamal was born in the United States but his mom was born in Jamaica, so her **background** is different from his.*

facts (fakts) *noun*   **Facts** are pieces of information that can be shown to be true.
EXAMPLE: *To decide what kind of dog to get, Jeralyn's family looked up **facts** about different breeds in a dog encyclopedia.*

interview (IN tuhr vyoo) *noun*   In an **interview,** a person asks another person a series of questions.
EXAMPLE: *Efrain's favorite singer answered questions about herself during a TV **interview**.*

understand (uhn duhr STAND) *verb*   To **understand** is to know the meaning of something.
EXAMPLE: *I am able to **understand** some Spanish words because I am studying Spanish in school.*

What should we learn?

Sports teams are made up of people who are not alike. However, all good sports teams are alike in one way. They put aside differences to achieve success. As you read the article, ask yourself: **How do people who are different learn to work together?**

THE TITANS REMEMBER

CRASH! A brick flies through a window. The brick is a hate message to a coach at T. C. Williams High School. If you saw the movie *Remember the Titans,* you probably cannot forget that scene. Coach Herman Boone, played by Denzel Washington, was the first African American head coach of the school's football team.

In real life, the attack was even worse. It was not a brick that smashed Boone's window. It was part of a toilet. In an **interview,** Boone said, "I've never gotten over that incident. . . . I could never **understand** how anybody could feel so bad about another human being as to throw a toilet . . . through a window."

TRUE TO LIFE? This happened in 1971, when race relations in the United States were changing.

▲ **Denzel Washington as Herman Boone, coaching the Titans at football camp**

In many areas, black students and white students were going to the same schools for the first time. At T. C. Williams High School in Alexandria, Virginia, the biggest change did not take place inside the school. It took place outside, on the football field. Coach Boone worked with white coaches to build a championship football team. Their story was so inspiring that moviemakers filmed it almost thirty years after the fact.

After the movie's success, some people tried to **analyze** how well the movie told the story of the real 1971 Titans. Players on the real-life team reported that parts of the movie exaggerated the **facts.** Some of the relationships between players were not as tense as they are in the movie. Some scenes in the movie never happened in real life. Also, some movie characters were made-up.

> Coach Boone said, "I forced them to be a part of each other's [life]."

REAL-LIFE LESSONS Though not all of the movie is **factual,** it does tell some important truths. The film is about teens who learn to work together in spite of differences in their **background,** and the real Titans did just that. Over time, whites and blacks began to see each other for who they were, not for what color their skin happened to be. Not all the teammates became friends. However, they did learn to respect one another's differences. Then they put aside those differences to become a winning team.

One key to the team's success was going away to training camp rather than training on school grounds. Coach Boone brought the team to Gettysburg College for a week so that they would have to spend a lot of time together. At the training camp, the teammates practiced together, learned together, ate together, and started to communicate with one another.

In the end, the teammates built an **understanding** of each other. "I forced them on each other," Boone says. "I forced them to learn each other's culture. I forced them to be a part of each other's [life]."

WE ARE BROTHERS One of the saddest scenes in the movie takes place when player Gerry Bertier is paralyzed in a car accident. In the movie, the accident happens before a championship game.

In real life, Bertier was injured while driving home on the night of the school sports dinner. What happens next in the movie, however, is based on **fact.** When Bertier's teammates came to see him in the hospital, nurses told them only family members could visit him. The players—both black and white—really wanted to see Bertier to show their support for him. To get around the family-only rule, the players told the nurses that they were Bertier's immediate family members. Perhaps the nurses were moved by the players' loyalty to him and one another. In the end, the nurses decided to let the players visit their fallen teammate.

The Titans of 1971 have always remembered the lessons they learned that season. They have carried those lessons forward to today. To show support for the students of T. C. Williams High School, the members of the Titans "family" created the Titan Foundation. Their goal is no longer to win a championship. Now their goal is to offer college scholarships to deserving seniors at T. C. Williams. It is a very fitting way for the Titans of 1971 to be remembered.

WRAP IT UP

Find It on the Page

1. Who is Coach Herman Boone?

2. What did someone throw through Coach Boone's window in the movie? What did the person throw in real life?

3. Contrast the real story of the Titans with the filmed story. How do the stories differ?

Use Clues

4. What about the story of this football team makes it a fitting subject for a movie?

5. If you could interview Coach Boone, what questions would you ask him and why?

6. Do you think it is OK for a movie about real people to change facts and events? Explain why or why not.

Connect to the Big Question

After reading this article, what would you say is the key to helping people who are different learn to work together?

Real-Life Connection

How much do you know about the U.S. space program? Find out by telling which of the following inventions you think came out of the program:

1. Microwave ovens
2. Video-game controls
3. Smoke detectors
4. Throwaway diapers

Check It Out

The U.S. government spends about $17 billion a year on the space program. Since the early 1970s, the space program has focused on building a space station that orbits high above Earth. The space station provides a place to do scientific research about outer space. In the future, it may allow people to travel farther into space.

WORD BANK

examine (ig ZA muhn) *verb*   When you **examine** something, you look at it very carefully.
EXAMPLE: *Please **examine** the book to see if any of the pages are torn or missing.*

experiment (ik SPER uh muhnt) *noun*   An **experiment** is a test to find out new facts or to show that old facts are true.
EXAMPLE: *In science class, we did an **experiment** to see which type of bean grows the fastest.*

explore (ik SPLAWR) *verb*   When you **explore** a place, you look it over carefully in order to learn more about it.
EXAMPLE: *I was able to find all my classrooms because I had a chance to **explore** my new school before the first day of classes.*

investigate (in VES tuh gayt) *verb*   When you **investigate** something, you find information about it in order to understand it better.
EXAMPLE: *Our job was to **investigate** the history of our school.*

What should we learn?

Like many people, you might know very little about the U.S. space program. You might be surprised by what everyday conveniences got their start as space technology. You might also be surprised by the program's cost. As you read the article, ask yourself: Is the information we gain from space exploration worth the cost?

THE PRICE OF DISCOVERY

Death came without warning on the bright morning of February 1, 2003. Seven astronauts had spent more than two weeks on the space shuttle *Columbia*. High above Earth, they were only minutes from landing. Suddenly, there was a bright flash in the sky. The shuttle broke into thousands of pieces.

Right away, scientists began to **investigate** why the shuttle had failed. One major theory is that a piece of foam that had fallen from the shuttle during lift-off damaged some of the shuttle's heat protection tiles, which led to the explosion.

After the *Columbia* disaster, some Americans' attitude toward the space program began to change. In the 1960s, when astronauts first went into space, many Americans wanted to **explore** outer space. That desire still held in 1969, when American astronauts landed on the moon.

A CHANGE IN ATTITUDE Most Americans support space **exploration,** but some changed their minds and attitudes when the National Aeronautics and Space Administration (NASA) changed their plans.

▲ On January 16, 2003, *Columbia* made its final lift-off at the Kennedy Space Center.

In 1971, NASA decided to end American flights to the moon. NASA decided to focus on building a space station instead. The station would orbit high above Earth, and astronauts would travel to it in space shuttles. The first shuttle flight took place in 1981.

Since then, more than a hundred flights have taken place. Two of the flights ended in disaster. Fourteen astronauts lost their lives. As of this writing, the space station is still not finished. It will probably not be finished until 2010 or later.

HIGH COST The total cost of the space station will be more than $100 billion. Though other countries are helping to pay the cost, some Americans think the cost is still too high. A single space shuttle flight can cost more than $1 billion. The bottled water used on the space station costs almost $500,000 per day! (For more information about NASA's spending, see the chart on this page.)

NASA SPENDING	
Year	Spending (in $)
2005	15,613,000,000 (actual)
2006	15,554,000,000 (estimated)
2007	16,356,000,000 (estimated)

Information is from the United States Office of Management and Budget.

Some scientists believe that NASA made a mistake. They think the space program should not have changed its direction to focus on the space station. In fact, in 2005, the head of NASA said, "It is now commonly accepted that was not the right path." He added, "Had the decision been mine, we would not have built the space station."

MUCH TO GAIN On the other hand, many people still argue that the space program has been worth the cost. They point out that the space station has given us ways to **explore** how people might survive on other planets someday. For example, scientists have done an **experiment** on ways to grow plants in space. They have also **experimented** with ways to produce oxygen from available water. In addition, they have been able to **examine** how outer space affects the human body. This information will help future settlers in space stay healthy. It also increases their chances of a successful settlement.

People in favor of space **exploration** also point out that many practical inventions have grown out of the space program. For example, the robotic arms used in the medical field today were first made for use on the space station. Technology used in ear thermometers was first developed to detect the birth of stars. Many people wear sunglasses that were first made to protect the eyes of spacecraft workers. Space program **experimentation** has also led to the fire-resistant material that is used to make suits for firefighters.

Thanks to cameras made for use in outer space, we have clear maps of our entire planet. We can also thank the space program for satellite radio and satellite TV. Even the joysticks we use on video games are based on tools made for space travel.

NEW DIRECTION In 2004, NASA decided that it would start sending missions to the moon again by 2020. The space shuttle program will end in 2010. Many people are happy with the new plan. Others still think the cost of the space program is too high.

NASA director Michael Griffin disagrees. He says that he wants space **exploration** to continue "for the American people, for my grandchildren, for my great-grandchildren."

WRAP IT UP

Find It on the Page

1. What happened to *Columbia* on February 1, 2003?

2. According to the article, how did most Americans feel about the 1969 moon landing?

3. How did the space program change after 1971?

Use Clues

4. Why do some people say the space program is too costly?

5. How has the space program benefited people?

6. Do you agree with the NASA decision to send missions to the moon by 2020? Explain.

Connect to the Big Question

After reading this article, do you believe we can learn enough from space exploration to justify its cost? Explain your answer.

Real-Life Connection

What do you know about dangerous jobs in the United States? Find out by writing whether you think each idea below is true or false.

1. Trash collection is one of the ten most dangerous jobs.
2. Each year, almost 6,000 people are killed on the job.
3. For most workers, the most dangerous part of their job is traveling to work.
4. Dangerous jobs are the highest-paying jobs.

Check It Out

Fishing for a living is almost always a dangerous job. One of the most dangerous fishing jobs is crab fishing off the coast of Alaska. Boat crews head out into freezing water and work with heavy machinery in terrible weather conditions.

WORD BANK

curiosity (kyoor ee AH suh tee) *noun*   When you have **curiosity** about something, you have a strong interest in learning about it.
EXAMPLE: *Blair's **curiosity** about his new neighbors led him to knock on their door.*

discipline (DI suh pluhn) *noun*   A **discipline** is a subject or a field of study.
EXAMPLE: *Lali's favorite **discipline** is math because she enjoys working with numbers.*

discover (dis KUH vuhr) *verb*   When you **discover** something, you find it or learn about it for the first time.
EXAMPLE: *The first time that Latrel played the drums, he was surprised to **discover** that he was naturally good at playing them.*

inquire (in KWYR) *verb*   When you **inquire** about something, you ask questions about it.
EXAMPLE: *Elaine decided to **inquire** about the cost of tickets for the concert.*

question (KWES chuhn) *verb*   When you **question** something, you challenge the truth of it.
EXAMPLE: *Guillermo's story was so strange that I began to **question** whether he was telling the truth.*

What should we learn?

Many people work under dangerous conditions for little pay or thanks, yet their efforts make life a little easier and more enjoyable for the rest of us. As you read the article, ask yourself: **What can we learn from people who do dangerous jobs?**

SOMEONE HAS TO DO IT

You would freeze to death very quickly if you fell into the icy waters of the Bering Sea. Waves taller than buildings might toss your boat around like a toy. Ice might coat the decks and railings. On the slippery boat, you would have to pull 750-pound metal traps from the water. Be careful! Your legs might get caught in the ropes attached to a trap. If they did and the trap slid back into the water, you would disappear into the dark, freezing depths.

You might lose your life working on a crab-fishing boat off the coast of Alaska. However, chances are good that people who eat crab legs at their favorite restaurant do not have the **curiosity** to **inquire** about how the food got to their plates.

HELP WANTED Many people would be surprised to **discover** how much danger there is in supplying the needs of everyday life. Look at all the things around you that are made of wood.

These workers are fishing in cold, dangerous weather off the coast of Alaska.

Next, look at all the things that use electricity. Finally, think about what you ate at your last meal. Everything you saw and ate is connected to a worker doing a dangerous job. The wood started out as part of trees, which are cut by loggers. In 2006, loggers had the third most dangerous job in the United States. Loggers risk being killed by falling trees and branches every day.

Power lines bring electricity into your home and school. In 2006, power line workers had the seventh most dangerous job in the United States. Every day, they risk falling from great heights or being electrocuted.

If your last meal was seafood, people may have risked their lives to catch it. People who fish for a living had the most dangerous job in the United States in 2006. They often work in terrible weather, far from land. One mistake can cost somebody's life. If you did not eat seafood, workers may still have faced danger to produce the food you did eat. Farm and ranch workers risk their lives to grow and raise food. One mistake with heavy equipment can be deadly.

THE TEN MOST DANGEROUS JOBS IN THE UNITED STATES
1. Fishers and Fishing Workers
2. Aircraft Pilots
3. Loggers
4. Iron and Steel Workers
5. Refuse and Recyclable Material Collectors
6. Farmers and Ranchers
7. Electrical Power-Line Workers (Installers and Repairers)
8. Roofers
9. Drivers (Truckers and Salespeople)
10. Agricultural Workers

Information is from the U.S. Bureau of Labor Statistics.

MOST DEADLY PLACES Each year, almost 6,000 U.S. workers are killed on the job. Though this number might come as a shocking **discovery** to many people, it is not surprising to workers with dangerous jobs. One place is particularly deadly for U.S. workers: the road. Truckers who transport many things all over the country had the ninth most dangerous job in the United States in 2006. The workers who drive garbage and recycling trucks had the fifth most dangerous job in the United States. Traffic accidents take their toll.

Are you **curious** about another dangerous workplace? It is the air. The second most dangerous job is that of airplane pilots. The pilots most at risk are not those who fly big airline jets. Rather, they are the pilots who fly small planes that spray crops or carry supplies.

WHY TAKE RISKY JOBS? Some people **question** the wisdom of doing dangerous jobs. Why take a job that could cost you your life? In some cases, people have no other choice. Loggers and farm workers might live in places where there are few other jobs.

In other cases, people follow older friends and older family members into jobs. For example, people who fish for a living often come from the same family or small community where fishing is a way of life. "[My] roots stem from a very small town off the coast of Norway," says a captain of a crab fishing boat. "My great grandfather and grandfather were fishermen in Norway, [so] it carries through."

In still other cases, people choose risky jobs because they do not want to be stuck in an office in front of a computer screen all day. They want a **discipline** that lets them be active or outdoors.

Of course, money is another reason that some people choose to take dangerous jobs. The fact is that some dangerous jobs pay better than other jobs that are not dangerous.

You may never risk your life for a paycheck. However, no matter what job you do someday, your life will probably be touched in some way by a worker who has a dangerous job.

WRAP IT UP

Find It on the Page

1. What is the most dangerous job in the United States?

2. Why is logging such a dangerous job?

3. Briefly summarize the reasons people decide to work at dangerous jobs.

Use Clues

4. Why may the road be such a dangerous workplace?

5. How would you make one of the dangerous jobs safer?

6. If you had a chance to do one of the dangerous jobs described, would you take it? Explain.

Connect to the Big Question

After reading this article, what do you think you can learn from people who do dangerous jobs?

Real-Life Connection

Many people have strong fears. On a chart like the one below, write an *X* in the box that tells how much you fear each thing listed.

I Fear . . .	A Lot	A Little	Not at All
Heights			
Closed spaces			
Insects			
Public speaking			

Check It Out

A phobia (FOH bee uh) is a strong, unreasonable fear. One of the most common phobias is arachnophobia (uh rak nuh FOH bee uh), fear of spiders.

approach (uh PROHCH) *noun*   An **approach** is an organized way to do something or to get somewhere.
EXAMPLE: *My **approach** to doing my homework is to follow a schedule.*

evaluate (i VAL yuh wayt) *verb*   When you **evaluate** someone or something, you form an opinion based on what you know.
EXAMPLE: *Lia had to **evaluate** the danger quickly when she saw the bear walking toward her.*

experiment (ik SPER uh muhnt) *noun*   An **experiment** is a test to find out new facts or to show that old facts are true.
EXAMPLE: *To come up with a low-fat dessert, my mom and I did an **experiment**: We used fat-free ingredients to bake.*

information (in fuhr MAY shuhn) *noun*   If you have **information** about something, you know the facts about it.
EXAMPLE: *Ed could not finish his report until he got more **information** from the library.*

knowledge (NAH lij) *noun*   **Knowledge** refers to all of the information and ideas that you have learned.
EXAMPLE: *Helping care for my little brother has given me the **knowledge** I need to be a good babysitter.*

What should we learn?

It is normal to be afraid of certain things. However, what happens to someone whose life is controlled by fear? Many people have this problem. As you read the article, ask yourself: How can people learn to overcome phobias?

HAVE NO FEAR

EEK! A SPIDER

This girl has arachnophobia, or the fear of spiders.

Kim was terrified of spiders. Just imagining the hairy legs, the beady eyes, and the pincer jaws made her sick to her stomach. Her heart jumped into her throat when she thought about spiders sucking fluids from flies trapped in webs. Moreover, looking at webs made her feel sick. She would not go into the attic or the basement. She was afraid she might see a spider in some dark corner. She could not go into any room without feeling afraid.

Kim's feelings about spiders might seem silly to you. However, for millions of people with arachnophobia, her feelings are no joke. These people have the same fear of spiders that Kim does. This fear is what mental-health experts call a phobia. Psychologists believe that phobias affect up to 10 percent of the people in the United States. Even when these people have enough **information** to know that they should not be afraid, they are still afraid.

FEAR IS NORMAL According to mental-health experts, fear is a normal and necessary emotion. Small children may be afraid to be left alone by their parents. Poor swimmers fear deep water—and they should.

Sudden loud noises scare almost everyone. The **knowledge** that something is dangerous is actually helpful. A healthy fear of strange dogs can keep people watchful. People who cannot swim are smart to **evaluate** the places they go to that are around water.

Fear is so normal that our bodies have a set way of reacting to it. Our hearts beat faster. We breathe faster, too. Because blood is pumping, we begin to sweat. Sometimes we might feel dizzy or sick to our stomach.

▲ **This close-up of a wolf spider shows its stare.**

WHEN FEAR TAKES OVER Mental-health experts say that many people can fight their fears. For example, people who fear giving speeches in front of other people can try a little **experiment.** They can practice speaking in front of a mirror or in front of small groups. Over time, their fear will lessen. Similarly, people who fear deep water may get over their fear by becoming strong swimmers.

Some people with phobias, however, have a harder time overcoming their fears. These people may have had a frightening experience that has left a strong "fingerprint" on the brain. For example, a child who accidentally locks herself in a closet may grow up with a deep and long-lasting fear of closed spaces. A child who is bitten by a dog may grow up so frightened of dogs that just the thought of one can cause an extreme reaction.

In the 1930s—a particularly difficult time in the United States—President Franklin D. Roosevelt gave a speech in which he encouraged Americans not to fear the future. "The only thing we have to fear is fear itself," said Roosevelt. In many ways, people with phobias are controlled by "fear itself." In fact, some people are fearful of becoming fearful. These people do not want to lose control in front of others, for fear of looking foolish.

FIGHTING PHOBIAS The good news about phobias is that they may not last. In fact, through **experimental** studies, psychologists have found ways for people to get over phobias. In general, the most effective **approach** is to use small steps to help people gradually get over their fears.

The first step is usually to look at things that a person fears the least about the subject of their phobia. For example, a person who has a phobia about spiders might look at a photograph of a spider from a long distance. That way, the spider looks smaller and less dangerous to the person.

The next step might be looking at spiders in a backyard. Then the person's therapist might suggest that the person sit in an empty room with a spider that is easily seen. Next, the person might watch another person pick up and hold a spider. These "baby steps" might lead to the person's letting a harmless spider walk on his or her arm.

At each step, the therapist **informs** the person about taking deep breaths to relax and stop fear from taking over. The therapist might give the person calming words to say when he or she feels too fearful.

Kim used this technique, and she was able to conquer her phobia. In fact, she now has a special pet in a glass case in her den. It is a hairy tarantula, a spider as big as her hand.

WRAP IT UP

Find It on the Page

1. What is a phobia?

2. Why do experts say that fear is normal and necessary?

3. What is the main difference between a fear and a phobia?

Use Clues

4. Why may taking small steps with a therapist help people get over phobias?

5. If you had a phobia about horses, how might you use the step-by-step approach to overcome it?

6. Why might it be important for a person to overcome a phobia?

Connect to the Big Question

After reading this article, how might you help a close friend who has a phobia?

PROJECT: Poster

Answer the Big Question: What should we learn?
You have read about different things that people learn—and why those things might be important to know. Now, use what you learned to answer the Unit 3 Big Question (BQ).

UNIT 3 ARTICLES

Travel to Mars,
pp. 76–79

Look Who's Talking,
pp. 80–83

Making Sport of Tradition,
pp. 84–87

In Your Dreams,
pp. 88–91

The Titans Remember,
pp. 92–95

The Price of Discovery,
pp. 96–99

Someone Has to Do It,
pp. 100–103

Have No Fear,
pp. 104–107

STEP 1: Partner Up and Choose
Your first step is to pick Unit 3 articles that you like.

Get together. Find a partner to work with.

Read the list of articles. Discuss which articles listed on the left side of this page were the most interesting to you.

Choose two or more articles. Pick articles that you both agree on.

STEP 2: Reread and Answer the Unit Big Question
Your next step is to answer the Unit BQ with your partner.

Reread the articles you chose. As you read, think about the Unit BQ.

Answer questions. For each article you chose, answer these questions:

- What in this article relates to the topic of learning?
- According to the article, what is important to learn?
- Why is this information important to learn?

Take notes. Use the information you took from the articles to answer the Unit BQ: What should we learn?

STEP 3: Discuss and Give Reasons
During this step, talk about your answer and start your poster.

Discuss your answer to the Unit BQ. Think about what is important to learn, according to these articles. What images or words could you add to a visual display about the Unit BQ?

Start collecting items to display on your poster. You might write quotations from the article and collect pictures from Web sites and print materials. For the article "Travel to Mars," for example, you might include a photo of the surface of Mars. For "Have No Fear," you might collect images that have to do with phobias.

STEP 4: Find and Add More Examples

Now, finish your poster.

Think more deeply about the Unit BQ. Discuss with your partner how you would answer the Unit BQ from your own point of view. What do *you* think we should learn?

Add more examples to the poster. Include examples that tell what each of you thinks is important to learn.

STEP 5: Check Your Work

Next, you and your group will look over your poster to see if you can improve it.

Use the rubric. Use the questions to evaluate your work. Answer each question yes or no.

Discuss your evaluations. Use the rubric answers as a guide to improve your work. You might rearrange items, add more color, add more specific ideas, and so on.

Finish the poster. Use ideas from your evaluation discussion to finish your work. If time and resources allow, you might create a multimedia presentation to showcase images and sounds that relate to your answer
to the Unit BQ.

RUBRIC
Does the poster . . . • clearly show the answer to the Unit BQ? • have words or images that relate to ideas in the articles? • include words or images that relate to ideas from the lives of both partners? • have an appearance—including color, layout, and number of images chosen—that viewers will find interesting and easy to understand?

STEP 6: Practice and Present

Get ready to present your poster to classmates.

Practice what you want to say. You will use ideas reflected on your poster to explain your answer to the Unit BQ. Think about what you will need to say. Each of you should handle one part of the presentation, but you can practice together.

Present your poster. Tell your answer to the Unit 3 BQ to your classmates. Explain clearly how the items on the poster answer the question. If you chose to do a multimedia presentation, introduce your answer before showing your work to classmates. Be prepared to answer questions.

What is the best way to communicate?

Two people can use more than two ways to communicate—and use them all at the same time! Cell phones, newspapers, Internet— which of these is the best way to communicate? Maybe the *way* you communicate depends on *what* you are communicating. As you read the articles in this unit, think of the different ways we communicate and ask yourself: Which way is the best?

Think about all of the ways you communicated on a typical day this week (for example, by phone, speaking, writing, e-mailing, text messaging, and body language). Jot them down. How long is your list?

Real-Life Connection

Giving and getting greeting cards is a pleasant part of life. What if the greeting card business folded? Copy the statements below. Write if you agree or disagree with each one to help answer the question.

1. I enjoy getting greeting cards.
2. I like funny greeting cards best.
3. I think paper greeting cards are a waste of paper.
4. I like to give greeting cards.

enrich (in RICH) *verb*   To **enrich** something is to add to it to make it better or richer than it was.
EXAMPLE: *Our teacher showed us some beautiful paintings to* **enrich** *our knowledge of art.*

entertain (en tuhr TAYN) *verb*   When you **entertain** people, you hold their interest by what you say or do.
EXAMPLE: *Beck tried to* **entertain** *us by telling a funny story about his uncle's fishing trip.*

express (ik SPRES) *verb*   To **express** yourself is to use words, images, or movement to communicate your thoughts or feelings.
EXAMPLE: *Tela wrote a poem to* **express** *her feelings of being alone in a new country.*

produce (pruh DOOS) *verb*   To **produce** something is to make it.
EXAMPLE: *The family built a factory to* **produce** *bottled water.*

translate (trans LAYT) *verb*   When you **translate** something, you say it in another language or another way.
EXAMPLE: *I selected a French dictionary from the library to help me* **translate** *the words.*

What is the best way to communicate?

You've got mail—real mail, that is. The return address says it is from a friend who moved away. You open it. Inside is a card with a printed message your friend has signed. There is no other note. What is your friend trying to say? As you read the article, ask yourself: **Are greeting cards a good way to communicate feelings?**

Thinking of You

*Y*ou get a greeting card for your birthday. Maybe it is funny, and it makes you laugh. Maybe there is a nice message inside that rhymes. Either way, someone took the time to pick a card out and send it to you.

People use greeting cards to **express** feelings and keep in contact with other people. They send cards for holidays or birthdays. They send cards when someone starts a new job or has a baby. They send cards when people get married. Cards are sent and received for just about any reason you can imagine. There are even cards for buying a new car. All these cards cost money. Some greeting card companies are big businesses. You have to wonder whether these businesses will last, though, now that computers and e-cards are common.

HOW GREETING CARDS BEGAN Notes of greeting have been around a long time. Some of the first greeting cards we know of were Valentines. As far back as the 1400s, people gave Valentine cards to one another. The first cards were handmade, and each one was unique. At one time in history, paper was very expensive, and only a few people could read and write. Before paper Valentines became popular, people said or sang their **expressions** of love.

How do you pick greeting cards?

People in Germany gave New Year's greeting cards as early as the 1400s. They made woodcuts of the greetings and printed them on handmade paper. These early cards were works of art. You do not need to **translate** them from German to appreciate their beauty.

HOW GREETING CARDS DEVELOPED While early greeting cards were handmade and hand delivered, as printing and mailing became less expensive, commercial cards became more popular. Printers began to **produce** more and more greeting cards. Mass **production** brought the prices of cards down. Lower prices **translated** into higher sales.

▲ **Printed greetings and e-cards have replaced handwritten notes.**

One of the first U.S. printers to make greeting cards was Louis Prang. He began printing cards in Boston in the 1870s. Many consider Prang to be the founder of the greeting card industry in the U.S.

During the 20th century, the greeting card business in the U.S. began to grow. During World War II, companies made cards for people to send to soldiers overseas. In the 1950s, funny greeting cards with short punch lines became popular. Funny cards might **express** less serious emotions than other cards because their purpose is to **entertain.** During the 1980s, card companies branched out even further, creating cards for all kinds of occasions—from getting a new pet to "graduating" from kindergarten. Then, in the 1990s, a new kind of greeting card was developed.

The 1990s were **enriched** by the World Wide Web. Greeting card companies started making Web sites that offered electronic cards, or e-cards. Today, you can choose from thousands of free e-cards. Many include movements and sound effects.

MORE CHOICE THAN EVER Today, more than 90 percent of households in the United States buy greeting cards. You can spend several dollars on a card, or you can send an e-card for no money at all. You can send a card that tells how you feel, or you can send a card that is purely **entertaining.** You can send greetings for a special reason or for no reason at all. Whatever you are thinking, there is likely to be a card to match it.

The paper greeting card industry is worth billions of dollars each year. Surprisingly, the introduction of e-cards has not hurt those sales. In fact, according to an employee of one of the big card companies, "What consumers are telling us is they really like cards of any sort." E-cards are "just one more way for them to communicate, to surprise the people they love and care for."

Psychiatrists say that the best communication is face-to-face communication. Seeing your facial **expression** and hearing your voice is the easiest way for someone else to understand your true meaning. Sometimes, however, it can be difficult to find the right words. Other times, the people we care about are far away.

When it comes to communication, doing what is best depends on the situation. Of course, whatever the situation, there is probably a greeting card for it.

WRAP IT UP

Find It on the Page

1. What were the first two kinds of greeting cards?

2. List three ways that paper cards and e-cards are alike.

3. Briefly state the main idea of the section titled "More Choice than Ever."

Use Clues

4. Where would you look to find an animated card that makes noise?

5. What do you think the next big change in greeting cards might be?

6. Which is better—a paper card or an e-card? Why?

Connect to the Big Question

After reading the article, how well do you think a greeting card works as a form of communication?

Real-Life Connection

Your cell phone is ringing. What if you are in a theater, seeing a movie? What if you are at school? Copy the chart below and add your thoughts.

Cell Phones	
What Is Good About Them	**What Is Bad About Them**
keep in touch	can interrupt things

Check It Out

Read on for some facts about cell phones.

- More than 200 million people have cell phones in the United States.
- Most cell phones have clocks, calculators, calendars, and games.
- Some cell phones can be used for text messaging, surfing the Internet, playing MP3s, or taking photos.

WORD BANK

communicate (kuh MYOO nuh kayt) *verb*   To **communicate** is to give or receive information.
EXAMPLE: *Robert can **communicate** well through his writing.*

listen (LI suhn) *verb*   When you **listen,** you pay attention to what you are hearing.
EXAMPLE: *In order to **listen** closely to the song, she closed her eyes.*

prepare (pri PER) *verb*   When you **prepare**, you get ready to use or to do something.
EXAMPLE: *Jared laid out his clothes to **prepare** for school the next day.*

technology (tek NAHL uh jee) *noun*   **Technology** is the use of science to solve real-life problems. It is also devices developed from this use of science.
EXAMPLE: *Jude uses computer **technology** to run his new business.*

transmit (trans MIT) *verb*   To **transmit** a message is to send it, often through a wire or radio waves.
EXAMPLE: *Alexander Graham Bell discovered how to **transmit** his voice through a telephone wire.*

What is the best way to communicate?

You have a cell phone in class. You forgot to turn it off, and it is ringing. Your teacher looks at you. Do you answer the phone? Do you let it ring? Do you turn it off, hoping your teacher forgets he heard it? As you read the article, ask yourself: **Do cell phones belong in school?**

Word on the Wire

Are cell phones toys or necessities? Do they belong in school at all? Many schools have banned their use in class. The ringing upsets lessons. Some students may play games or send text messages when they are supposed to be paying attention.

Maybe school leaders just need to **communicate** cell phone rules better and take phones from students who do not use them correctly—or maybe not. Some schools have had to ban cell phone **technology** altogether. Why? Students have used cell phones to cheat on tests. The phones can be expensive and easy to steal, so crime can rise when phones are allowed.

Some people suspect that cell phones interfere with learning on other levels as well. Students use them to **transmit** text messages to friends. Texting is quiet, but it is hard to **prepare** a text message and **listen** closely to a teacher at the same time. People who text leave out letters to save time and space, and that habit may hurt the users' abilities to spell and write well.

"The ability to write successfully is probably the most important skill for kids to learn in relationship to job success," according to a doctor at Baylor College of Medicine.

Cell phones are a convenient way to keep in touch, but they can be disruptive, too.

"If texting inhibits them from learning how to write articulately, then it could be a real problem."

What do you think? Do problems that can result from cell phone use outweigh the benefits? If you have ever seen someone texting in a roomful of people, you know he or she may not be talking or **listening** to the people nearby. Texting allows people to be connected, but the **communication** takes place at a distance.

GOOD SIGNALS Cell phones have many good points. Many people say they cannot get along without their phones anymore. The need to **communicate** seems to be growing. During much of the twentieth century, many homes had one phone. Family members took turns using it. Cell phones help us reach out much more than we might otherwise. Because texting is easy, people are writing to one another more than ever.

Cell phones also provide a measure of safety. Families and friends have a way to stay in contact almost anywhere. The phones are a good way for people to call for help in emergencies.

Transmitting text messages lets you make contact when friends and family cannot talk with you directly. It feels good to get and send text messages, and messages made with **preparation** show that you care. What could be wrong with something that makes you and others feel good?

PHONING IT IN Maybe phones and related **technologies** belong in schools, as tools of education. The media have started using text messages for ads. Movie companies send messages that tell what is new at the movies. Radio stations text **listeners.** What if teachers sent homework reminders this way?

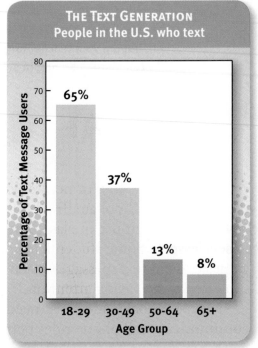

THE TEXT GENERATION
People in the U.S. who text

Information is from Mobile Marketing Association, 2006.

With wireless connections, some phones let you find directions when you get lost. You can look up important facts. Cell phones have many uses that were invented only recently. Should schools be teaching students how to sift through the bad uses and get the most from the good?

WHAT IS NEXT AFTER TEXT? Early cell phones were almost as big as shoeboxes. As time has passed, though, cell phones have gotten smaller. Have you ever seen someone you thought was talking to herself and then realized she was on a hidden phone? Cell phones continue to shrink and take on more uses.

What might be next? Some people think we will have chips implanted in our brains that we will be able to use to do what cell phones do. You might be able to **transmit** messages to other people. Given that phones are used for advertising already, you might have a constant stream of ads running through your head.

Will **communication technology** become even more a part of us? If so, should schools be teaching the right way to use it? Are schools right to ban this technology? What do you think?

WRAP IT UP

Find It on the Page

1. Give three reasons for banning cell phones in school.

2. What two school skills can text messaging hurt?

3. List one positive and one negative use of cell phones.

Use Clues

4. What is one way to solve the problem of cell phone use in school?

5. What are some reasons people give for being unable to get along without their cell phones?

6. How could cell phones and text messaging be used in a good way in the classroom?

Connect to the Big Question

After reading the article, what is your opinion of cell phones in the classroom?

Real-Life Connection

Not all heroes have superpowers and live in comic-book worlds.
Copy the word web below and jot down your thoughts on heroes.

```
  ⬭             ⬭
        Hero
  ⬭             ⬭
```

WORD BANK

contribute (kuhn TRI byuht) *verb*   To **contribute** is to do or give something to reach a goal.
   EXAMPLE: *Kiri wants to **contribute** $10 to the fund for the firefighters.*

inform (in FAWRM) *verb*   When you **inform** people, you communicate information or knowledge to them.
   EXAMPLE: *Sarah had to **inform** her teacher that she would be moving in a week.*

react (ree AKT) *verb*   You **react** when you take action in response to another action.
   EXAMPLE: *Elias had to **react** to the strong wind by holding his hat on his head.*

source (sawrs) *noun*   A **source** is a place where something begins.
   EXAMPLE: *One **source** of the river is a spring that pours out of the ground.*

speak (speek) *verb*   When you **speak,** you use your voice to talk.
   EXAMPLE: *Henry wanted to **speak** to the younger kids about his love of reading.*

What is the best way to communicate?

A sudden rainstorm dumps tons of water upriver. The river rises quickly, and soon it will flood. Your friends are camping near the water. You do not know if they heard the warning. Should you risk trying to find them or just hope they stay safe? As you read the article, ask yourself: **How do real-life heroes show courage?**

A Show of Strength

You might not think the following people would have much in common. Jeremy was a twenty-year-old counselor at a gym in Minnesota. Wesley was a fifty-year-old construction worker in New York City. Alize was a twelve-year-old student in Maryland. What they had in common was their courage. All three risked their own lives to save the lives of others. Each one is a hero. Here are their stories.

A BRIDGE COLLAPSES A bus was carrying children on a field trip in Minneapolis. The vehicle was crossing a bridge when suddenly the bridge collapsed. The bus slipped downward three times and then teetered on the edge of the broken structure. At any moment, the bus was going to fall into the water below.

How did the riders **react**? Jeremy Hernandez was seated toward the back of the bus. He kicked the back door open and handed children to rescuers outside the bus. He helped save fifty-two children. The accident happened fast, so Hernandez had to **contribute** fast.

▲ **Part of a Minneapolis bridge collapsed during rush hour on August 1, 2007.**

When asked to **speak** about it later, he said, "I feel good for what I did. I just— I think it was more adrenaline than anything because I was in fear of my life, too, so that's what made me kick into action."

For Hernandez, the catastrophe was a **source** of fear, but the fear did not paralyze him. He later said his heart was beating fast, and he feared for his own life. In spite of his fear, he stayed on the bus until all the children were safely off.

▲ **Jeremy Hernandez speaks about his experience.**

A MAN FALLS ON THE TRACKS Wesley Autrey was waiting for the subway with his two young daughters when a young man near them became sick and fell onto the tracks.

Witnesses would later **inform** the press that Autrey automatically went to the rescue. He jumped down to pull the man to safety. A train was coming, so there was no time to get off the tracks. Autrey pushed the young man down between the rails as the train passed over them. Five subway cars passed over the two men before workers could turn off the power and stop the train.

"I don't feel like I did something spectacular," Autrey said when he **spoke** about the ordeal. "I just saw someone who needed help. I did what I felt was right."

The train passed within inches of Autrey and the young man. "I had to make a split decision," Autrey later said. He decided to save the life of a stranger.

A HOUSE BURNS One day, Alize Spry's mother ran out for milk. Alize was left in charge of her four younger siblings. However, she was soon put to a very scary test. There was a fire.

The smoke alarm went off, and Alize **reacted** quickly. She took the children to a bedroom on the second floor, because there was too much smoke and heat for them to get out of the house. From there, Alize called 911 and spoke calmly, **informing** the operator about the family's situation. The operator told her to get everyone down on the floor, which she did. When firefighters arrived, they found the children immediately. By then, however, several of the children had passed out from the smoke. The firefighters pulled them through a window to safety and revived them. Things could have been much worse. Alize's quick thinking and actions had saved the children's lives.

"I thought I would never see my sister, my brother, and my parents again," she said later, "and I just tried the best I can to just do something."

FACING THE UNPLANNABLE It is good to have a plan for escaping your house in case of fire and to take safety courses in case of an emergency. However, you cannot plan for everything. Each disaster is unique. Somehow, these heroes looked inside themselves and found a **source** of courage when they needed it most. They may have been driven by fear or the desire to live. They might have thought that what they were doing at the time was the only action that made sense. Their stories have **contributed** to our understanding of courage. They showed that heroes are not just in storybooks. They live among us.

WRAP IT UP

Find It on the Page

1. Give the names and ages of the three heroes mentioned in this article.

2. Summarize how each of these people showed courage and became a hero.

3. Briefly state the main idea of the section titled "Facing the Unplannable."

Use Clues

4. What can we learn from these three stories of heroism?

5. What evidence in the article supports the idea that sometimes heroes are scared?

6. Which person profiled in this article do you think was the most heroic? Why?

Connect to the Big Question

After reading the article, how do you think real-life heroes show courage? Explain your answer.

Real-Life Connection

Most people make just enough money to get by or to live a comfortable life. Very few make a lot of money. Why do some people make so much more money than others—and is anyone worth it? To help you decide, write whether you agree or disagree with each of these statements.

1. People should be paid according to their worth.

2. People should be paid according to the importance of their jobs.

3. People should be paid according to how entertaining they are.

4. All people should be paid the same amount, no matter what they do.

WORD BANK

entertain (en tuhr TAYN) *verb*   When you **entertain** people, you hold their interest by what you say or do.
EXAMPLE: *Sophie tried to **entertain** us by telling jokes, but no one was in the mood to laugh.*

media (MEE dee uh) *noun*   The **media** is all the types of communication that reach many people, such as newspapers, TV, or radio.
EXAMPLE: *Jay gave his story about the missing dog to the **media**, and we heard it reported on the news.*

teach (teech) *verb*   To **teach** is to explain information or to show how to do something.
EXAMPLE: *I want to **teach** my cousin how to swim, but she will not even get into the pool.*

transmit (trans MIT) *verb*   To **transmit** a message is to send it, often through a wire or radio waves.
EXAMPLE: *Morse code uses a system of dots and dashes to **transmit** a message.*

What is the best way to communicate?

Leo got straight A's in school. Now he is a science teacher. It is an important job. He works long hours and has special training. His friend makes much more money driving a race car. He takes big risks on the racecourse. As you read the article, ask yourself: **What message do we send with the salaries we pay to "stars"?**

The Big Money

In one recent year, the president of the United States made $400,000. That might sound like a lot of money, but a golfer named Tiger Woods made $90 million that same year. A certain talk show host topped them both by making $225 million. Can you guess the name of that host? That host is Oprah Winfrey.

In the United States, star power is often measured by the amount of money a person makes. Some stars play sports, some **entertain,** and some run businesses. In each case, stars are usually the best of the best at what they do and attract **media** attention. They often end up losing their privacy, which might be worth some kind of extra payment. Even so, why do stars get paid so much?

CHIEF AMONG THEM *CEO* stands for *chief executive officer.* CEOs run big companies. In 2005, the median salary among the CEOs of the country's 100 biggest companies was $17.9 million dollars.

Some people think CEOs deserve big salaries, because they run companies that employ a lot of people. Many CEOs have graduate degrees and special skills in business. Compared with other employees, they tend to work longer hours and have to take greater responsibility for risks.

Tiger Woods is one of the most popular ▶
pro athletes in the United States.

However, others point out that some CEOs get big money no matter how their company does. CEOs are often asked to leave poorly performing companies, yet they might get millions of dollars as they walk out the door. On the other hand, if a company does poorly, the average worker might lose the job.

Many VIPs can afford to travel in private jets.

STAR POWER Being good at your job is part of star power, but not all of it. Most children's authors do not make more money than other people do, even though some of them are very good writers. However, some books are especially loved. Perhaps this is because these books **teach** a powerful lesson. Perhaps it is because they tell a story in an interesting way. In either case, they can become blockbusters with movie and merchandise spin-offs. The authors of these popular books can become famous and make a lot of money.

Tiger Woods is an amazing golfer. He earned $90 million the same year the U.S. government paid the president only $400,000—about 200 times less than Woods made. Most people who play golf pay to play. For Woods, it is the other way around. He is fun to watch and extremely talented. Just his presence can **transmit** the idea that golf is more than merely a game. Still, some people ask how a person who hits a ball into a hole can earn as much as he does.

Many rappers have a great voice and sense of rhythm. Why are only a few superstars? How do you measure star power in terms besides dollars? Is it figured by the amount of space a **medium** like magazines gives to stories about a star? Is it the star's **entertainment** value?

HARD DOLLARS In some ways, stars decide how much their abilities are worth. They go after the money they want, and many work really hard for what they get. In other ways, however, we all decide who gets to be a star and what that person is paid. When you buy a CD, a ticket to a game, or a product, you can help make a star.

What about people who shine but are not in the public eye? **Teachers,** police officers, and social workers all work hard to make a difference in people's lives. Some people would say that these are the men and women on the front lines of the battle to help others. You can say an excellent basketball player is an inspiration to others, but is his or her contribution really the same thing?

The average salary of a U.S. store manager is $41,000. That store manager may be in charge of many people. Managing a whole store can be a big job. It includes working with both the store's employees and the store's customers. The CEO of the store's parent company can make hundreds and even thousands of times more money than a store manager makes. Is the work the CEO does hundreds of times more important than what the store manager does?

There are many factors at play when it comes to determining a salary. Different jobs require different skills and experience. What does the dollar value we put on some skills say about us?

WRAP IT UP

Find It on the Page

1. Which person mentioned at the beginning of the article made the least money?

2. How are CEOs, big entertainers, and star athletes all alike and different?

3. How are a teacher and a CEO alike? How are they different?

Use Clues

4. How do everyday people help make stars?

5. What conclusion can you draw about how we treat stars?

6. If you disagree with how much money a star makes, what can you do about it?

Connect to the Big Question

After reading the article, what message do you think we send by the salaries we pay stars?

Real-Life Connection

How do you keep money in your wallet? Do you work? Do you get an allowance?

Say you get an allowance, but it falls short of covering expenses. A good after-school job opens up. To keep getting an allowance, you must keep doing your chores. If you give up chores and allowance to work at the job, your money will still fall short. Do you give up free time to work? Do you stick with just the allowance, or do you work, too? Write your thoughts.

WORD BANK

contribute (kuhn TRI byuht) *verb*   To **contribute** is to do or give something to reach a goal.
EXAMPLE: *Each member of the art club is asked to **contribute** a monthly fee to help pay for supplies.*

copy (KAH pee) *verb*   To **copy** something is to make another one that is exactly the same.
EXAMPLE: *I asked to make a **copy** of Kristi's notes, because I missed science class last week.*

learn (luhrn) *verb*   You **learn** when you get new information or knowledge about a subject.
EXAMPLE: *I want to **learn** enough of the Spanish language to live in Spain someday.*

produce (pruh DOOS) *verb*   To **produce** something is to make it.
EXAMPLE: *Henry Ford made a factory to **produce** cars.*

relate (ri LAYT) *verb*   When you **relate** information, you tell a story or describe an event.
EXAMPLE: *Fritz tried to **relate** the exciting parts of the baseball game to his friends.*

What is the best way to communicate?

Think of all the stuff you want. Now, think of how you get it. Usually, you get things by using money. You learn how to manage money by handling money. As you read the article, ask yourself: What do families communicate by paying kids an allowance?

Pay Days

People used to think a person went straight from being a child to being an adult. Both periods of life tended to be short. During the last century, however, people started living and working longer. These new facts of life **produced** a new concept—that there is a special period of time between childhood and adulthood. People began seeing the teen years as a time to enjoy **learning**—a time to be given responsibility and asked to **contribute** something but not too much.

As a teen, you can probably **relate** to being both an adult and a kid. One of the tough aspects of the teen years is getting money to fund your adventures. There is no doubt that teens spend money. Gretchen Marks, vice president of marketing at Coinstar, **relates** this fact: "Teens are the fastest-growing consumer segment today, spending $170 billion [in 2002]."

JUST FOR BEING YOU Some families provide an allowance to help their kids **learn** to manage money. You might get $10 a week. At that rate, it could take a while to save for a video game, and that is the point.

Many young people earn an allowance by doing chores.

Learning to save is part of learning money management. Some families make a rule that money must be saved from every allowance. Others believe it is important to give to charity, so they make a rule that teens must **contribute** part of their allowance to charity.

It is often easier to **learn** things by doing them instead of just hearing about them. It can also be easier to **learn** the right way of doing something if you **copy** the behavior. To **learn** to paddle a canoe, it is good to try **copying** someone else's motions. If you apply the same idea to money, it makes sense for older family members to give younger ones an allowance and be there to help manage it.

Providing an allowance is one thing. Tying the allowance to work is another issue. Not everyone agrees that kids should work for allowances. Some family leaders think that giving allowances for chores teaches kids that the only reason to work is to earn money. To make life worthwhile, they say, it is important to work for another reason besides money.

Young people may be **learning** something negative, however, when their allowances are not tied to work. They may expect money to come in regularly whether they work for it or not. Do you know the old saying, "Money doesn't grow on trees"? If kids think they deserve money just for being who they are, they will probably be in for a big shock when they grow up.

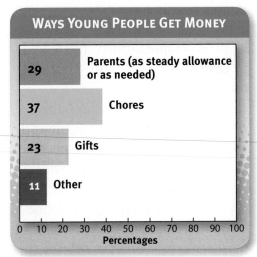

WAYS YOUNG PEOPLE GET MONEY

- 29 — Parents (as steady allowance or as needed)
- 37 — Chores
- 23 — Gifts
- 11 — Other

Percentages

Information is from GfK Roper Consulting, *2005 GfK Roper Youth Report.*

TIED TO CHORES Some families think it is important to teach teens to work for money. They want teens to get in the habit of **relating** financial success to making an effort or to **producing** something. These families think that tying an allowance to work is the best way to prepare young people for the real world. Doing that does teach an important lesson. However, there can be a down side to working for an allowance as well.

To some people, getting paid an allowance and doing chores seem like two separate concepts. To them, getting an allowance for doing chores gives young workers the wrong idea. These people believe that kids should do chores because the kids are part of a family, not because they will make money. Also, kids who do not care about money may refuse to do paid chores.

ON THE JOB How do most teens get money? A recent report showed that, on average, teens earn about $30 a week—from doing chores and other jobs, getting an allowance, and receiving gifts. In another report, almost three-fourths of teens surveyed said they do odd jobs, and more than one-third hold down a regular or part-time job. Some people, however, are against the idea of teens working. They think it is more important to do schoolwork than earn money. What do you think? Can teens **learn** anything useful at a job?

Teens spend money on items that are popular, such as fashionable clothes and entertainment. Some teens do not get enough allowance to buy what they want. They may choose to get jobs rather than spend less money.

What **contribution** do families make to their teens' **learning** by not giving enough allowance? What **contribution** do they make by giving too much?

WRAP IT UP

Find It on the Page

1. What difficult aspect about being young does this article discuss?

2. What is the main reason families give allowances?

3. Summarize the section of this article titled "Tied to Chores."

Use Clues

4. What might result if no teens received allowances?

5. What hard evidence shows that people disagree on which method of giving an allowance works best?

6. What is your opinion of teens' spending habits?

Connect to the Big Question

After reading the article, what message do you think families communicate by paying teens allowances?

Real-Life Connection

Music can make us laugh, cry, love, hate, rebel, or go to sleep. Every generation has its own music. What is yours? Copy the chart. Place an *X* in the appropriate box to show how much you know about each type of music.

Type of Music	Know a Lot	Know a Little	Know Nothing
Jazz			
Rock and Roll			
Country			
Folk			
Reggae			
Hip-Hop			

WORD BANK

describe (di SKRYB) *verb*   When you **describe** something, you communicate the details about it.
EXAMPLE: *Luis drew a picture to help **describe** the bike he wanted to build.*

enrich (in RICH) *verb*   To **enrich** something is to add to it to make it better or richer than it was.
EXAMPLE: *He added whole grain to **enrich** the bread.*

express (ik SPRES) *verb*   To **express** yourself is to use words, images, or movement to communicate your thoughts or feelings.
EXAMPLE: *Tina sang a song to **express** her sadness.*

listen (LI suhn) *verb*   When you **listen,** you pay attention to what you are hearing.
EXAMPLE: *Allie wanted to **listen** to the words of the song, so she closed her eyes.*

reveal (ri VEEL) *verb*   When you **reveal** something, you uncover or show something that was hidden.
EXAMPLE: *Cho opened his hand to **reveal** the necklace he held.*

What is the best way to communicate?

The words *mood* and *music* go together. No matter how you feel, there is music to fit your mood. Music can help create moods, too. It can set a mood and send a message. As you read the article, ask yourself: **When music takes different forms, does it send different messages?**

The Music Mix

When you hear the word *salad,* what do you picture? How about just lettuce and tomatoes with dressing on top? That was the standard mix in the 1950s, but having so few ingredients is considered plain now. Today, many diners **enrich** their greens with meat, cheese, seeds, and more.

In the same way, the word *music* means something different today from what it meant in the 1950s. Back then, hip-hop had not even been invented yet. Other forms of music, like heavy metal, were also unheard of then.

Three important ingredients in all music are rhythm, melody, and harmony. Another word for rhythm is *beat*, and another word for melody is *tune*. You get harmony when you combine different musical sounds. The music you hear now mixes the main ingredients differently from the way the music of the 1950s mixed them. Today's top musicians have tossed in new ingredients for **enrichment. Listeners** have new kinds of music to enjoy and even new ways of experiencing it.

Louis Armstrong is one of the most famous Jazz musicians of all time. ▶

SIGN OF THE TIMES One of music's main jobs is to **express** feelings, but it can **describe** a time and place, too. If you **listen,** the same music may **reveal** something new each time you hear it. The more musicians **listen** to other musicians, the more music changes. One **revelation** invites another.

For hundreds of years, folk and classical dominated the music scene. Then, recorded music came along, making it easier than ever for different regions and musicians to share sounds. Since then, music has taken on many new forms, changing with the times.

Rock and roll was born in the 1950s from several types of music, including rhythm and blues. Basic rock and roll then took on different forms, including surf music, folk rock, and psychedelic rock. Some folk songs of the 1960s protested the Vietnam War and promoted civil rights and basic human freedoms. During that

▲ New types of music often emerge with new types of dance.

same time, soul singers blended voices in smooth **expressions** about both hard times and good times. In the mid-1970s, disco music became popular. Many people just wanted to dance.

In the past thirty years, people have **listened** to country, punk rock, reggae, and heavy metal. They also have **listened** to industrial, new wave, grunge, and techno music. Each type of music has its own rhythm, melody, and harmony. Every musician leaves his or her own stamp on the music.

HIP-HOP AND BEYOND Hip-hop has been a major development and influence on the music scene. It originated in the predominantly African American South Bronx neighborhood of New York City in the late 1970s. Deejays would mix and manipulate records to create new sounds. Since the 1970s, hip-hop has grown from an urban U. S. sound to an international one.

Hip-hop became an experience that includes deejaying, "B-boying," and "MCing." Deejaying involves combining sounds, scratching records, and more. "B-boying" is a form of break dancing. "MCing" is rapping, talking, and entertaining the audience with words.

Although hip-hop and folk rock have different origins and different sounds, they address some of the same concerns. Some hip-hop songs protest issues of racism and poverty, which were also protested in some folk songs of the 1960s.

STOMP *Stomp* is a musical show that began in England in 1991. The people in the show do not sing. They dance and move and stomp. They use everyday objects to make music. Here is how one critic **described** the show: "The cast challenge each other as they layer beats that sort of make you forget they are making music from toilet plungers . . . garbage can lids . . . even the kitchen sink!"

The sounds of *Stomp* are music in a new form, offering a new listening experience. What will be next in music? Have you heard something new? Is the next big thing already happening near you?

WRAP IT UP

Find It on the Page

1. To what does this article compare music?

2. What are three main ingredients of music?

3. What did recordings do for music?

Use Clues

4. What conclusions about our society can you draw by looking at how music has changed since the 1950s?

5. How do you think music will change in the future?

6. Which kind of music do you think is the best, and why?

Connect to the Big Question

After reading the article, what do you think about today's music? When music takes a different form, does it send a different message?

Real-Life Connection

Have you ever watched a fish swimming in a fishbowl? You can see it from just about any angle. You can watch everything it does. The life of a celebrity is often called "life in the fishbowl."

Imagine if your life was like that. Copy the following chart and then write your thoughts about the good and bad sides of being a celebrity.

Good	Bad

WORD BANK

media (MEE dee uh) *noun*   The **media** is all the types of communication that reach many people, such as newspapers, TV, or radio.
EXAMPLE: *The story was soon all over the **media**.*

method (ME thuhd) *noun*   A **method** is a certain way of doing something.
EXAMPLE: *Kelli had her own **method** of making popcorn in the microwave.*

paraphrase (PER uh frayz) *verb*   You **paraphrase** when you reword something spoken or written, usually to make the meaning clear.
EXAMPLE: *Sam tried to **paraphrase** Martin Luther King Jr.'s famous "I Have a Dream" speech.*

react (ree AKT) *verb*   You **react** when you take action in response to another action.
EXAMPLE: *Elias had to **react** to the strong wind by holding his hat on his head.*

technology (tek NAHL uh jee) *noun*   **Technology** is the use of science to solve real-life problems. It is also devices developed from this use of science.
EXAMPLE: *My **technology** teacher told me I have a way with computers.*

What is the best way to communicate?

Where did your favorite actor eat dinner last night? What cause is the hot couple supporting this week? Where did your favorite athlete go on vacation? Many people know the answers to these questions. As you read the article, ask yourself: What does people's fascination with celebrity life communicate?

Follow Your Star

Have you ever followed the stars? Following a star today often means picking up a magazine or logging on to a fan Web site. It means turning on the TV or reading a newspaper gossip column. So many people seem obsessed with celebrities' lives these days. What does that fact say about these people?

NATURAL STARS You have probably heard of alpha dogs. An alpha dog is one all the other dogs in a pack follow. Long ago, people learned to follow the leader as a **method** of protecting themselves. Often the leader was a warrior or a king or queen. According to one psychologist, people naturally take a keen interest in "the ones who are important in the pack."

Then modern **technology** came along, and the **media** got involved. Today, people follow celebrities' lives as if the celebrities were their leaders. A star's face grows familiar, and people **react** to the star as to a friend. Joyce Brothers, a psychologist and a celebrity, says, "Our prehistoric brains haven't caught up with TV."

For some celebrities, fame means giving up their privacy.

Unit 4 **137**

To **paraphrase** what Brothers said, the **media** and related **technologies** make many of us feel close to alpha people we have not met.

The private lives of celebrities are made public through every **medium** there is. That is because celebrity news is one of the **methods media** companies use to hold our attention. Martha Nelson, the former managing editor of *People* magazine, explains that people need to socialize. They love to gossip, but in today's world, people sometimes do not even know their neighbors. "So, celebrities," she explains, "become the common focus of gossip."

What kind of magazine news are you drawn to?

FALLEN STARS According to social historian Daniel Boorstin, celebrity satisfies "our exaggerated expectations of human greatness." In the past, heroes were known for the great things they did. Today, the famous are known by their images. Heroes used to be self-made, but today, the **media** helps make them. Once, our heroes came from history books, sacred books, and folk stories. Today, they are people who live among us.

How did this happen? **Paraphrasing** a recent *Newsweek* article by Sean Smith: After September 11, 2001, our news became more serious. However, at the same time, media coverage of celebrities has exploded. Could it be that many of us focus on celebrity gossip to avoid thinking about more serious concerns?

Psychologists think it is OK to be interested in the lives of celebrities if that interest does not replace relationships in our own lives. In a recent study, researchers found that a third of the people surveyed qualified for something they called "celebrity worship syndrome." For the worst sufferers of this condition, a celebrity has become central to their lives. Some of them might think of the celebrity as a good friend. People with this syndrome are more likely to suffer from depression or low self-esteem than other people are.

FOLLOW THE LEADER Many people copy celebrities as a **reaction** to fame. Celebrities tell us what to wear, what to buy, and what to eat and drink. They make a lot of money doing it. Celebrities who have alcohol and drug problems, however, set bad examples. So do celebrities who act like two-year-olds. Celebrities who develop eating disorders in an effort to stay slim set bad examples, too. Then there are the stars who land in jail.

Why are people still interested in celebrities even after they fall? Maybe seeing celebrity problems can make people feel better about themselves and their own problems.

Some celebrities, however, use their status to set good examples. "Celebrities can have a positive influence on our life," says a professor of psychiatry at Mt. Sinai School of Medicine. "They can be very helpful in terms of increasing awareness and decreasing stigma about many problems, including health problems."

Some celebrities take their roles seriously and do good work around the world. Looking at all the "stars" you know, do you think some deserve their status? Does their behavior affect which ones you follow?

WRAP IT UP

Find It on the Page

1. Why do people want to follow a leader?

2. In two different ways, compare and contrast heroes of past times with today's celebrities.

3. What is "celebrity worship syndrome"?

Use Clues

4. What effect does the media have on people's obsession with celebrities' lives?

5. How could you change the influence celebrities have over you?

6. What is your opinion of the use of celebrities in advertising? Explain your answer.

Connect to the Big Question

After reading the article, what do you think people's fascination with celebrity life communicates about these people?

Real-Life Connection

What is your sport? Whatever it is, you might dream of turning pro, playing for a few years, and then retiring at age thirty. If those events happened, what would you do for the rest of your life? Write your response.

Check It Out

- A hundred years ago, life expectancy at birth was only about fifty years but today it is much higher.
- As athletes age, they tend to lose flexibility and coordination, but they tend to gain in areas that help in endurance sports: pacing, strategy, and strength of mind.
- The Summer National Senior Games have been held every two years since 1987.

WORD BANK

argue (AHR gyoo) *verb* When you **argue,** you give reasons for or against an idea.
EXAMPLE: *Santos and his brother often argue about who should take the garbage out.*

inform (in FAWRM) *verb* When you **inform** people, you communicate information or knowledge to them.
EXAMPLE: *They used signs to inform the people in the neighborhood about the lost dog.*

learn (luhrn) *verb* You **learn** when you get new information or knowledge about a subject.
EXAMPLE: *It was hard to learn anything with all the noise going on in the room.*

speak (speek) *verb* When you **speak,** you use your voice to talk.
EXAMPLE: *The candidate stayed after the meeting so she could speak to the reporter.*

teach (teech) *verb* To **teach** is to explain information or to show how to do something.
EXAMPLE: *She had to teach them a few manners before taking them to the fancy restaurant.*

THE BIG ?

What is the best way to communicate?

At age seventy, bodybuilder Jack LaLanne swam more than a mile wearing handcuffs while towing seventy people in seventy boats. LaLanne stayed fit well into his nineties. Most athletes retire much younger, however. As you read the article, ask yourself: **What message about aging do older athletes communicate?**

The Age Factor

Jim Morris is the hero of one of the greatest baseball stories ever—so good, it is the subject of a book and a movie. Morris played a lot of baseball as a kid and dreamed of becoming a big-league player. He was even drafted into the minor leagues when he was twenty-four, but his run at his dream did not last long. By the time he was twenty-eight, Morris was out of professional baseball because of arm injuries.

Morris got married, went back to college, and began raising a family. He settled down to **teach** high school science and to coach baseball.

THE MAJOR LEAGUES When Coach Morris was thirty-five, he made an important **speech**. He stood up to **speak** to his baseball team about working hard and following their dreams. In response, his team challenged him: If they won their district championship, Coach Morris would have to try out with a Major League Baseball team. He would have to follow his own advice.

Jim Morris's story inspires many to reach for their dreams.

The team ended up winning their championship, and Coach Morris held up his end of the bargain. He went to a Major League tryout, where the seemingly impossible happened. He threw twelve 98-mile-an-hour pitches in a row.

The Tampa Bay Devil Rays would soon **inform** the **teacher** that they wanted him. Morris pitched for the Devil Rays and in his first game he struck out an all star player with a 98-mile-an-hour fastball. He lived the dream as long as it lasted—until his shoulder began bothering him.

Morris retired from baseball but not from **teaching.** He started **speaking** to audiences about following their dreams. People go to listen to him, because they know they can **learn** something.

> Information on eating right and staying fit is keeping athletes healthy longer than ever.

IS 40 THE NEW 25? Older athletes are still a novelty, but advancements in sports medicine have opened up new possibilities. **Information** on eating right and staying fit is keeping athletes healthy longer than ever. You still play even as you get older.

Add the lessons that older athletes have **learned** through years of playing their sport. You get well-rounded athletes who can make good decisions as they compete.

Through a seventeen-year career in the Canadian Football League, Danny McManus made more than 50,000 passes. "My body has changed, and maybe my style of game has changed," he said about being almost forty and still playing, "but the number-one factor in continuing to play is, it's still fun to play the game."

Who wins by **arguing** against him? As an older, wiser player, McManus said, "You understand your position is that of a pro football player, and you're more strict with yourself. Your body is your office."

OUT WITH THE OLD? Although aging athletes can take care of their bodies, their abilities still decline. They might still be good compared with most people, but does it always make sense for them to keep playing? Would their time and effort be better spent training younger people?

Look at Brett Favre, the Green Bay Packers quarterback. By 2007, he had played for the Packers for 16 years. From 1994 to 1996, he threw 110 touchdown passes. From 2004 to 2006, Favre threw 68 touchdown passes. Many fans began to wonder if Favre was just getting too old to play the game well. The 2007 season turned all that around. On December 16, 2007, at the age of thirty-eight, Favre set a new NFL record for most career passing yards.

When asked about the 2007 season, Favre said, "I have to look at: Can I still play at a high level? I believe that. I still feel like I have something to give to the team. The Packers feel like I can lead this team." Favre was not ready to give up. His body was not ready to give up. Perhaps most importantly, his team was not ready to give up on him.

It is easy to **argue** that as athletes age, they should leave gracefully. They should go out at the top of their game. You can also make the **argument** that they should stay as long as they can. They should stay as long as it is fun for them. If older players are still making contributions, why should they not continue to play?

WRAP IT UP

Find It on the Page

1. Why did Jim Morris try out for the Major Leagues at age thirty-five?

2. List three reasons why older pro athletes should be valued.

3. What does "Your body is your office" mean?

Use Clues

4. What conclusions can you draw from the stories of McManus, Morris, and Favre?

5. How could you connect the story of Jim Morris to someone you know?

6. How would you evaluate the abilities of an older athlete compared with those of the same athlete at a younger age?

Connect to the Big Question

After reading the article, what message about aging do you think older athletes communicate?

PROJECT: TV Commercial

Answer the Big Question: What is the best way to communicate?

You have read articles that discuss communication. Now, use what you learned to answer the Unit 4 Big Question (BQ).

UNIT 4 ARTICLES

Thinking of You,
pp. 112–115

Word on the Wire,
pp. 116–119

A Show of Strength,
pp. 120–123

The Big Money,
pp. 124–127

Pay Days,
pp. 128–131

The Music Mix,
pp. 132–135

Follow Your Star,
pp. 136–139

The Age Factor,
pp. 140–143

STEP 1: Form a Group and Choose

Your first step is to pick Unit 4 articles that you like.

Get together. Find a small group to work with.

Read the list of articles. Discuss which articles listed on the left side of this page were the most interesting to you.

Choose two or more articles. Pick articles that you all agree on. Write their titles on separate pieces of paper for note taking.

STEP 2: Reread and Answer the Unit Big Question

Your next step is to answer the Unit BQ with your group.

Reread the articles you chose. As you reread, think about the Unit BQ.

Answer questions. For each article you chose, answer these questions:

- What kind of communication is described in the article?
- Is this method of communication one of the best ways to communicate? Why or why not?

Take notes. You will answer the Unit BQ in a TV commercial, selling your answer to viewers. Begin brainstorming ideas.

STEP 3: Discuss and Give Reasons

Discuss reasons that will help you "sell" your Unit BQ answer.

Discuss your answer to the Unit BQ. Give reasons based on things you read in the articles. Answer questions like these:

- What kind of communication is described in the article?
- What is good about this kind of communication? Do these qualities make this communication the "best"?

Summarize your answers in a plan for a commercial. Go over your notes and underline or circle ideas that you want to include in your commercial.

STEP 4: Create Your Commercial

Now, make a final plan for your commercial.

Get a grabber. Think of the best way to grab your audience's attention. How will you make sure they are watching or listening?

Create a script for the commercial. Be sure each group member has a part in the commercial. Write a script—the words each group member will say. Think about how you can convince your viewers that one form of communication is the best. Use language that will persuade them.

STEP 5: Check and Fix

Next, you and your group will check your commercial to make it even more convincing.

Use the rubric. Use the questions to evaluate your commercial script. It will be easier to evaluate if you read it aloud together.

Discuss your evaluations. If you answered no to any question, think of what you need to do to answer yes. If you need help from another group, listen to each other's commercial "practice" and answer the questions.

Improve your commercial. If your commercial could be more convincing or interesting, change the script so that audience members will "buy" your answer to the Unit BQ.

STEP 6: Practice and Present

Get ready to present your commercial.

Practice your commercial. Use your script to practice. You can write each person's part on a separate index card. Remember to use persuasive words and to show enthusiasm.

Present your commercial. It is time to perform your commercial. If you have time and resources, think about shooting a video of your commercial to show the class. You can use music, special effects, and so on to help sell your idea in a convincing presentation.

RUBRIC

Does the TV commercial . . .
- clearly answer the Unit BQ: What is the best way to communicate?
- include ideas from at least two Unit 4 articles?
- have a lively and interesting script that will grab audience members' attention?
- include persuasive language to "sell" your answer?

Do others see us more clearly than we see ourselves?

This student and his teacher have very different views of his art. Why might the student have trouble realizing how talented he is? As you read the articles in this unit, think about how other people may see you. Can your own ideas about yourself keep you from knowing who you really are?

Put yourself in the place of this student. How do you think he feels about his work now that his teacher has encouraged him? Why might the opinions of experts affect what we think of ourselves?

Real-Life Connection

Who are the most successful people you know? Think about what it took for them to be successful. What do talent, luck, and attitude have to do with success? Tell whether you think each of the following statements is true or false to see where you stand in your thinking about success.

1. A positive attitude guarantees winning at sports.

2. Most people hang out with others who have a similar attitude.

3. If you have a negative attitude, you will always fail.

4. You can learn to think positively even if you have always been negative.

characteristic (ker ik tuh RIS tik) *noun*   A **characteristic** is a trait that describes a person or thing.
EXAMPLE: *Optimism is a **characteristic** of enthusiastic fans.*

focus (FOH kuhs) *verb*   To **focus** is to concentrate on one thing.
EXAMPLE: *A safe driver has to **focus** on the road.*

perception (puhr SEP shuhn) *noun*   A **perception** is what you see or understand about things that happen around you.
EXAMPLE: *My **perception** of the movie is that it is too violent for little kids.*

reflect (ri FLEKT) *verb*   An action will **reflect** a belief when it demonstrates what a person is thinking.
EXAMPLE: *Trying to create less garbage can **reflect** an interest in helping the environment.*

setting (SE ting) *noun*   A **setting** tells where and when action takes place.
EXAMPLE: *The movie's **setting** is a small town in the Midwestern United States.*

Do others see us more clearly than we see ourselves?

"You should try out for the talent show. You are so funny, I bet you would do a great comedy routine!" "You think so? I would be too nervous." Have you ever been on either side of a conversation like this? Which side sounds more like you? As you read the article, ask yourself: **Do negative thoughts keep you down?**

How Attitude Helps

It has probably happened to all of us: We thought we did our best, but that test or assignment did not go as well as we thought it would. How would you react to this situation? You might decide, "This subject is too hard for me to learn." You could also think, "Next time, I'll **focus** harder on the material." Your reaction probably **reflects** your attitude toward many situations, not just those at school.

Why do some people **perceive** that things will always go wrong, while others assume all will turn out well? One athlete might worry that he will foul out in a game while a teammate **focuses** on dreams of a state championship—and makes those dreams come true.

Some people believe we are born with a certain kind of personality: negative or positive. You either look for the good in situations or **focus** on the bad.

◀ **Who do you think** ▶ **will be more successful?**

These people think we have little choice about the **characteristics** of our personality. They believe we cannot change what we were given.

SELF-HELP In 1952, a new book, Norman Vincent Peale's *The Power of Positive Thinking*, challenged the **perception** that our personalities are "set." Peale **characterized** successful people as upbeat. The message of the book was that positive thinking could change lives for the better. He insisted that people could change the way they **perceive** situations. According to Peale, a positive attitude is a choice.

The self-help industry earned $9.6 billion in 2005.

EMPOWERING People must have liked Peale's message, because his book stayed on the *New York Times* best-seller list for more than three years. Nearly sixty years later, people continue buying his and other self-help books. Television programs that **focus** on positive thinking appeal to many buyers and viewers. We are told that we can create a **setting** for success: Expect to succeed, and you will get good results. People who do not expect success are magnets for failure.

One guest on a talk show about empowerment explained that she had an easier life than her sister had. She felt guilty and would not let herself succeed. Then she decided to change her **character.** She made a list of things in her life that she could imagine being good. She gave up worrying about what was currently holding her back and rejected her old excuses. By taking a positive view, she seized power.

She directed her energy to a series of positive steps. She realized that her working for someone else did not **reflect** her abilities, so she developed a business plan and became her own boss. She turned her positive energy toward finding love. These efforts led to fulfilling other goals, including marrying, having a child, and buying a home. She had assumed she would succeed, and she did succeed.

Helen Keller is a famous example of how positive thinking works. An illness left her blind and deaf when she was a toddler. Still, she learned to read, speak, and even lecture to large crowds. Keller said, "We can do anything we want to do as long as we stick to it long enough." Her achievements are a **reflection** of such commitment.

TRUE FOCUS New self-help books appear every month. In fact, the self-help industry earned $9.6 billion in 2005. You might begin to wonder why new books and infomercials have to be created. Were the old ones not full of great ideas? Some people wonder if these media are helping people change, or if they are only helping the authors and talk-show hosts get rich.

MAKING YOUR OWN CHOICES What is your opinion about self-help media? Do you think it is possible for a person to control his or her own life just by thinking positively about goals? Do you think a book or television show can teach you how to set good goals and then follow through on them? Part of every success program is making choices. Usually, one of those choices involves listening to advice about improving yourself. You can get that advice from many sources. Some experts believe that success is in your own hands. They claim that you are not born with a winning attitude. Rather, you make it happen yourself. Negative thoughts just might chip away at your success. Positive thoughts, however, can create success.

WRAP IT UP

Find It on the Page

1. What book did Norman Vincent Peale write?

2. What is the difference between a positive personality and a negative personality?

3. Briefly summarize the goals that the woman on the talk show set and her results.

Use Clues

4. Why do some people who have positive goals fail?

5. Why might setting positive goals have negative effects?

6. What changes would make your own life more positive than it is?

Connect to the Big Question

After reading the article, do you think that negative thoughts are keeping you down? If so, how do you think you can change those thoughts to find a positive path?

Real-Life Connection

What do you think of when you hear the word *happiness*? What do you think makes people happier—to give or to receive? Use a word web like the one below to capture your thoughts about happiness.

Happiness

appreciate (uh PREE shee ayt) *verb*   To **appreciate** something means to value it.
Example: *My grandparents always **appreciate** help with chores around the house.*

complete (kuhm PLEET) *adjective*   Something that is **complete** has all of its parts or is finished.
Example: *I have a **complete** set of my favorite band's music and videos.*

define (di FYN) *verb*   To **define** something means to give its exact meaning.
Example: *It is the coach's job to clearly **define** the duties of each position on the team.*

ignore (ig NOHR) *verb*   To **ignore** something, pay no attention to it.
Example: *If you **ignore** the weather forecast, you might get stuck in a storm without the right gear.*

reaction (ree AK shuhn) *noun*   A **reaction** to something is a response to it or an effect of it.
Example: *Dad's **reaction** to his team's winning touchdown was to jump up and cheer.*

THE BIG ?

Do others see us more clearly than we see ourselves?

You forget to bring your lunch to school, so a classmate offers you half his sandwich. You smile gratefully, but you notice that he is smiling as well. He is giving up part of his lunch, so why is he so pleased? Maybe the act of sharing made his day. As you read the article, ask yourself: **What does it take to be happy?**

Happiness: A Two-Way Street?

▲ **Volunteers for Habitat for Humanity receive joy from building homes for others.**

Have you ever heard the saying "Happiness is a two-way street"? People who believe this idea find **complete** happiness in making others happy. Is giving a new trend? Why are so many people taking part in it?

BUILDERS AND ANGELS Your eyes are glued to the television set. You cannot **ignore** watching a family in need receive a brand new house. A crew has spent a week demolishing and then **completely** rebuilding a home in bad disrepair. Major companies donated appliances and furnishings to make this house into a home. The work crew is exhausted, but each member is happy. The family's **reaction** is heartwarming. The companies that gave appliances and furniture for the project have their names on the screen. Are these companies looking for publicity, or do they just want to help? Why, do you think, are viewers drawn to stories like these?

You change the channel and see talk-show host Oprah Winfrey tell about her Angel Network. This organization encourages people to give money and time to help good causes. The efforts of Winfrey and Angel Network supporters help **define** a trend in helping others. The Angel Network supports projects around the globe.

These projects help people who might otherwise be **ignored.** One project is the **completion** of schools in rural areas. The Network has built thirty-four schools in ten struggling countries, including Ecuador, Ghana, and Haiti.

▲ Each time kindness is shown, a kindness movement grows.

Many people have spare coins under their couch cushions or stored in a jar. Winfrey challenged people to collect and give that spare change. So far, the Angel Network has raised more than $50 million. The "spare change" given by viewers of just one program about South Africa netted $9 million. Viewers **reacted** when they learned about the plight of victims of hurricanes Katrina and Rita. They gave more than $15 million to the Network's fund for hurricane relief.

KINDNESS MOVEMENTS Happiness can come from sources other than money. An organization called the Random Acts of Kindness Foundation (RAK) matches volunteers with charitable organizations that could use help. RAK publicizes charitable projects so that would-be volunteers recognize needs and find projects to suit them.

Some people give without being part of kindness movements. One couple founded a company and later sold it for a large profit. They had a lot to give, but they had spent their lives giving. The business owner **defined** one reason he worked hard: "I would use a large portion of the wealth created to try and make a difference for others."

FEEL-GOOD WORKERS Even major corporations are becoming part of a culture of giving. Some companies sponsor charities, while other companies give time or money without publicizing their gifts. Corporate sponsors have their names attached to their giving. Some people believe that these companies are involved in charitable work just to have their names out there for "doing good." Studies have shown, though, that such companies benefit in another way as well: Employees **appreciate** the giving and **react** positively. Why?

Some workers feel pride in knowing they are part of a company that gives back to its community. Other workers feel that their company's giving adds purpose and meaning to their work. They can choose to take part in company giving. Taking part helps them see themselves as more than just employees. Finally, company giving can help workers feel committed to a good cause. They can say to themselves, "That is our charity, and we can help out with it." Employees who feel that their work has purpose and meaning tend to be happier on the job than other employees. Many companies see benefits in helping charities and in involving their employees.

WHY DO WE GIVE? People give for many reasons. They might have extra money or time to share, or their **appreciation** for others' kindness to them might make them want to give back. Studies have shown that, in the long run, people feel more satisfied when they do something for others than when they do something just for themselves. In this case, happiness really is a two-way street.

WRAP IT UP

Find It on the Page

1. What does RAK stand for?

2. List two projects that Winfrey's Angel Network has done to help people in need.

3. Briefly summarize reasons that people might have for being involved in giving.

Use Clues

4. Why, do you think, does the Angel Network appeal to so many people?

5. What advice would you give to a company that wants to lift its employees' spirits by giving?

6. What changes might you make in your life to find more happiness than you have now?

Connect to the Big Question

After reading the article, what do you think it takes to be happy? Why, do you think, do people help others?

Real-Life Connection

Secrets bind people. A friend might tell you about a secret crush. Where is the harm in that? What if they tell you about a destructive behavior? Should you keep that secret? Draw and fill in a chart like this one.

If a friend . . .	I would . . .
abused alcohol or drugs	
was into self-abuse	
had an eating disorder	

Check It Out

Intervention is an attempt to change the behavior of another person.

- Scared Straight, an organization started in a New Jersey prison, is an example of group intervention. Organizers show prison life to teens so the teens know where destructive behavior can lead.

- In a personal intervention, friends or family members confront an individual, pointing out why his or her behavior worries them.

appearance (uh PIR uhns) *noun*   The **appearance** of a situation, place, or thing is its outward look.
EXAMPLE: *The dirty **appearance** of the restaurant scared them away.*

consider (kuhn SI duhr) *verb*   To **consider** options means to think about your choices carefully.
EXAMPLE: *Bill did not **consider** their feelings when he neglected to call.*

image (I mij) *noun*   An **image** is a mental picture of something.
EXAMPLE: *He would not like Jessica's **image** of him.*

perspective (puhr SPEK tiv) *noun*   One person's **perspective** is a special point of view in judging things or events.
EXAMPLE: *From Michael's **perspective**, the club was a waste of time.*

reveal (ri VEEL) *verb*   When you **reveal** something, you uncover or show something that was hidden.
EXAMPLE: *Jada would not **reveal** her choice for student government president.*

Do others see us more clearly than we see ourselves?

If a friend's cell phone is stolen, you offer sympathy. If a friend is stealing from people, sympathy will probably not help. Helping friends recognize hurtful behavior is hard, and it can backfire. Why bother, then? As you read the article, ask yourself: **Why might an intervention be the best way to help someone?**

CALLED OUT

Go to any crowded middle- or high-school lunchroom and take a look. Even if the group's **appearance** does not **reveal** anything alarming, problems lurk beneath the surface. If you could see each person's **perspective,** you would see that being young can be problematic. **Consider** the pressures even "good students" feel to keep up an **image.**

When under pressure, some people develop self-destructive behaviors. What can you do when those people are your friends? Should you back off, figuring it is best just to "live and let live"?

WHY INTERVENE? Intervention is an attempt to help people escape from harmful habits or threats. Sometimes, an organization like a school will do it. A counselor might call someone in for meetings, or administrators might suggest special programs. Other times, family members or friends take someone aside for a serious discussion.

No one is perfect, so knowing someone who is out of control and in need of help is normal. Maybe you have always assumed that individuals should figure out how to solve their own problems.

Teens face tough decisions each day.
▼

That is what growing up is, after all—learning to direct your own life. It can make sense to mind your own business. You might know only half of someone's story, and it might not be the right half!

Get help from people who know what to do.

Intervening may seem beyond your skills. No one likes to be "called out" for behavior. The person who needs help may be defensive or angry. When is looking the other way no longer an option, though?

PROBLEM BEHAVIORS Do you think a friend's personal problems are best left to experts? Do you believe that your friend's parents should do the work instead of you? These **perspectives** are logical, but they are not always helpful. Friends are often the first to notice when friends are spinning out of control.

You might have a friend who does not seem capable of having a good time unless he has tuned out with alcohol or drugs. Lately, you have not had fun when around him, and you are **considering** walking away from the friendship. You could have a friend who wanted to lose weight but has lost so much she is no longer healthy. Even so, she seems obsessed with her **image.** When she looks at herself in mirrors and pictures, she thinks she looks fat.

There are many calls for help: Maybe a friend starts spending almost all her time at home on the Internet, sending hurtful messages. Someone else seems depressed.

You could "live and let live." According to recent statistics, however, 68 percent of teens say they turn to friends or siblings when they face these kinds of problems. Your friends might go to you for help.

WARNING SIGNS Erratic behavior is a warning sign. Maybe you have a friend you used to be able to count on, and now she often breaks off plans. Perhaps you feel like a babysitter when you do get together.

Maybe a friend starts dropping classes, and his grades sink. A person is in crisis if neglected hygiene or a sudden shift in personality **appears, revealing** changes for the worse. If a friend becomes threatening or violent, it is time to do something to help.

INTERVENING Intervention is not one-size-fits-all. It can come in many different forms of plans and people who care. Intervention strategies range from training for kids and parents to short-term wilderness therapy programs, day treatment, or, in extreme cases, hospitalization or residential programs. "More than anything," says one expert, "the intervention must be appropriate to the level of risk."

Helpers need to realize that failed interventions may lead to more serious problems. Talk with a trusted family member, a teacher, a doctor, or the like—someone who seems likely to know how to navigate the process successfully. Together, you can form a team to confront your friend. Tell him or her you care and want to help. Give specific examples of ways the behavior has been hurtful. Tell your friend where help is available. After he or she gets help, be there to help support your friend.

WRAP IT UP

Find It on the Page

1. What is intervention?

2. List three warning signs that someone needs help.

3. Briefly summarize three situations that might cause teens to need help.

Use Clues

4. Why do only some teens develop problems that might need intervention?

5. Why might some interventions cause more problems than they solve?

6. What do you think could be done to help prevent at-risk kids from developing serious problems?

Connect to the Big Question

Someone says to you, "I have a friend with a serious problem. Do you think I should intervene?" What would you say?

Real-Life Connection

Some people would rather have other people say bad things about them than say nothing at all. How would you feel if you were the target of gossip, though? Have you ever been attacked online? To explore your views about online gossip, tell whether each of the items below is true or false.

1. People can say what they want. It is just words.
2. Victims of rumors always deserve what they get.
3. People who are bullied online would never bully others online.
4. Most online rumors turn out to be true.

WORD BANK

appreciate (uh PREE shee ayt) *verb*   To **appreciate** something means to value it.
EXAMPLE: *I appreciate when I get a ride to school and do not have to walk or take the bus.*

assumption (uh SUHM shuhn) *noun*   If you make an **assumption,** you suppose something is true without checking to make sure.
EXAMPLE: *Some adults make the assumption that kids are irresponsible.*

bias (BY uhs) *noun*   When you show a **bias,** you show a like or a dislike that prevents you from being fair.
EXAMPLE: *My neighbor has a bias against people with motorcycles.*

identify (y DEN tuh fy) *verb*   When you **identify** something, you recognize or describe it.
EXAMPLE: *After taking that summer class, I can identify every kind of tree in the park.*

reaction (ree AK shuhn) *noun*   A **reaction** to something is a response to it, or an effect of it.
EXAMPLE: *Her reaction to the rumor was disgust.*

Do others see us more clearly than we see ourselves?

When we trade stories with other people, we bond with them. Some people think that gossip can help them bond with others. Gossip can also be false and hurtful. As you read the article, ask yourself: What is the best way to handle hurtful gossip?

Pushing Buttons

WHO'S SORRY NOW? Not long ago, instant messaging and Internet social networks did not exist. If you wanted to talk with someone, you had to see the person or use the phone. It is easy to **identify** and **appreciate** the ways new communication technologies have improved life. We have more options than ever for keeping in touch. Even if you have grown up with online technologies, though, you may still feel a **bias** in favor of face-to-face or voice contact. It is easier to figure out people's **reactions** when you can see their faces or hear their voices in a conversation.

It is easy to misuse the new technologies. Some people spread negativity online, which does little to improve life for anyone. Others act as cyberbullies. They use the Internet to reach out and hurt other people.

CYBERBULLYING DEFINED

Cyberbullying involves threatening or attacking someone online. One expert has **identified** it as "willful and repeated harm inflicted through the medium of electronic text." Victims of

The Internet allows people to share information quickly. Not all the information is positive.

cyberbullying are more likely to call it confusing and hurtful. Cyberbullies try to control or to injure others with words. They do their dirty work with the **assumption** that a safe distance exists between them and their victims. Sometimes, victims know they are a target. Other times, they are unaware of what is happening.

Cyberbullies tease or torment a victim with e-mails, instant messages, or chat-room taunts. While some bullies "go public" by saying who they are, others hide their **identification.** This way, victims cannot trace their attackers. Some go public by posting their insults on online bulletin boards. Others have **biases** that run so deep they create special Web sites dedicated to destroying the reputations of their victims.

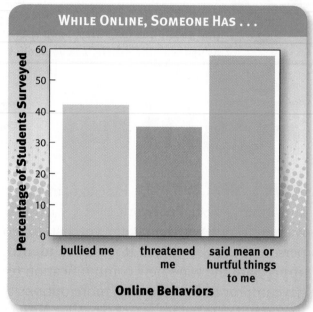

Information is from i-SAFE, *Cyber Bullying: Statistics and Tips,* 2004.

AMONG THE VICTIMS Why would anyone become a cyberbully? You should not **assume** there is any single reason. According to one expert, cyberbullies are "often motivated by anger, revenge, or frustration." Sometimes, they might post hurtful messages in an attempt to be entertaining. Other times, they might simply be responding to a posting without thinking their actions through. Then again, they might think they are righting a wrong. If you are the victim of a cyberbully, it makes sense to try to understand the bully's motivation so you can address the wrong in the right way.

Just as cyberbullies' motives vary, so do victims' **reactions.** A 2005 study found that about one third of all teens who responded said cyberbullying did not bother them. One third said it did bother them. Anger was the **reaction** cited by one third of the teens who responded. Many victims felt more than one emotion, and many said the bullying affected how they acted at home, at school, and with friends. Bullying could also affect how you act online.

If you are a victim, keep in mind that you have plenty of company. Many people will probably be ready to take your side. As more victims come forward, people take cyberbullying more seriously.

To protect yourself from cyberbullies and other Internet dangers, keep your private information private, advises one Internet safety group. If someone does something hurtful to you online, first take time to calm down. If you realize the hurt is more than you can handle, you can "stop, block, and tell." Stop communicating with the bully. Block the bully. Tell on the bully. Try to save other people from him or her.

QUESTIONS Do you believe that being teased is simply part of growing up? Do you think that it toughens people? What do you think of people who bully online? Are they cowards? If you or a friend were victimized by online gossip, what would you do?

Your answers to those questions probably depend on what has already happened to you. Some cyberbullies might not understand the harm they are doing. They might be repeating what other people did to them. Other bullies might believe that their actions teach victims how to get along with other people. The only good that comes from this form of bullying, however, might be a deepened **appreciation** for those who do not participate.

WRAP IT UP

Find It on the Page

1. Name three ways bullies spread rumors on the Internet.

2. List three emotional reactions that students had to bullying.

3. Briefly summarize ways victims of bullying can react.

Use Clues

4. Why do cyberbullies continue their online behavior?

5. Why might being a victim of bullying lead the victim to become a bully?

6. When does gossip cross a line and become harmful?

Connect to the Big Question

After reading the article, what do you think is the best way to handle gossip and bullying?

 PROJECT: # Write-Around

 **Answer the Big Question: Do others see us more clearly than we see ourselves?**

You have read articles that explore how we see ourselves. Now, use what you learned to answer the Unit 5 Big Question (BQ).

UNIT 5 ARTICLES

How Attitude Helps,
pp. 148–151

Happiness: A Two-Way Street?
pp. 152–155

Called Out,
pp. 156–159

Pushing Buttons,
pp. 160–163

STEP 1: Form a Group and Choose

Your first step is to pick Unit 5 articles that you like.

Get together. Find a small group to work with.

Read the list of articles. Discuss which articles listed on the left side of this page were the most interesting to you.

Choose two or more articles. Pick articles that you all agree on.

STEP 2: Reread and Answer the Unit Big Question

Your next step is to answer the Unit BQ in your group.

Reread the articles you chose. As you reread, think about the Unit BQ.

Answer questions. For each article you chose, answer these questions:

- What does the article tell us about how people might see themselves?
- According to the article, how might people see a person differently from the way the person sees herself or himself?
- How does this article help readers understand the influence that other people can have on us?

Take notes. Write the Unit BQ at the top of a sheet of paper for a write-around. Pass the paper around to group members. Each member has one minute to write an answer to the Unit BQ. Leave room after each response to add notes in step 3.

STEP 3: Discuss and Give Reasons

During this step, talk about your answer in your group.

Discuss the answers to the Unit BQ. Explain your answer to the group. Be sure to use details from the articles to explain your answer. Give each group member a chance to share his or her response. After each response, add to the write-around notes.

STEP 4: Summarize the Group's Response

Now, finish the write-around by creating a summary.

Reread your group's answers. Look over your notes and see if the members of your group generally agreed on the answer. Group members do not have to agree. If they disagree, the summary should give reasons for all points of view.

Summarize the write-around. Be sure that viewpoints are supported with reasons. Write the most important ideas from the write-around, not all of the ideas.

STEP 5: Check and Fix

Next, you and your group will look over your write-around summary to see if it could be improved.

Use the rubric. Use the questions to evaluate your work. Answer each question yes or no. You might trade summaries with another group to check their work and get another opinion about yours.

Discuss your evaluations. For your yes answers, think about what you can do to make your summary even stronger. If you have any no answers, talk about what you can do to turn each no into a yes.

Improve your summary. After discussing your summary by using the rubric, work together to make the summary stronger.

STEP 6: Practice and Present

Get ready to present your write-around and summary to classmates.

Practice what you want to say. You will use your write-around to explain your group's answer to the Unit BQ. You might have each group member present his or her answer. Then have one group member present the summary.

Present your work. Explain your answer to the Unit 5 BQ to your classmates. You might discuss it with them, or you might post your thoughts about the Unit BQ on a classroom Web page or in a blog.

RUBRIC

Does the summary . . .
- answer the Unit BQ?
- include details from at least two articles in Unit 5?
- show a clear relationship between the answer and the reasons given to support it?
- include the viewpoints of all group members, even if group members disagreed?
- show a clear organization by starting with the answer to the Unit BQ and then supporting that answer with details?

Community or individual— which is more important?

A community is a group of people, while an individual is just one person. Who does this teen seem to think is more important—her community or herself? This unit presents issues that involve communities and the individuals in them. As you read the articles, ask yourself: Is the community or the individual more important?

In what circumstances do you think a community could be more important than an individual? In what circumstances do you think an individual could be more important?

Real-Life Connection

Your school principal has just announced, "The dress code will change next term. Uniforms will be required." Would a strict dress code be good for your school? Would a stricter code cramp your style? In a chart like the one below, write what you think would be good and not so good about a strict dress code.

School Uniforms/Dress Code	
Benefits	**Drawbacks**

culture (KUHL chuhr) *noun*   A **culture** is the set of beliefs and habits that form a way of life for a group of people.
   EXAMPLE: *Celebrating special holidays is an important part of my family's **culture**.*

diversity (duh VUHR suh tee) *noun*   If a group has **diversity,** it is made of many different kinds of people or things.
   EXAMPLE: *My school has **diversity** among its students, who represent several races, ethnic groups, and religions.*

environment (in VY ruhn muhnt) *noun*   Your **environment** is made up of your surroundings.
   EXAMPLE: *My school provides a safe, fun **environment** in which students can learn.*

individual (in duh VIJ wuhl) *noun*   An **individual** is one person.
   EXAMPLE: *The Constitution of the United States protects the rights of every **individual** who is a citizen.*

Community or individual—which is more important?

Clothes are a great way to express yourself. They can also be distracting or make other people uncomfortable. For these reasons, school leaders want new dress code rules— now! You want an improved place to learn, but you also want to express yourself. As you read the article, ask yourself: **Is individuality more important than following the rules?**

The Great Dress Debate

By now you have figured it out: School is not just about reading, writing, and arithmetic. Your school experience can help you learn to be an **individual** and to fit into your community.

However, can the way you dress affect how well you and others learn? Some people think so. These people believe dress codes or uniforms can reduce violence and other problems at school. These people say they want to make schools safer and more serious about learning. Many students claim the right to wear whatever they like, though. They say dress codes and uniforms are obstacles to **individuality.** For these students, freedom of expression is more important than following rules. The debate raises this question: How do you keep a school **environment** safe while allowing students to be **individuals?**

SIGNS OF THE TIMES Look at a high-school yearbook from sixty years ago. The clothes kids wore back then might shock you! Clothing such as long skirts, dress pants, and neckties reflected the concerns of the time. In the 1950s, girls were not allowed to wear pants to class. In the 1960s, schools banned boys from wearing jeans.

What do you think of school dress codes?
▼

Schools measured the length of a girl's skirt and sent the girl home if it was too short.

When gang problems increased in the 1980s, many schools banned clothing and accessories that marked students as gang members. Some schools went further and adopted uniforms. While uniforms were common in private schools, the first public school to require uniforms was probably Baltimore's Cherry Hill Elementary, in 1987. Seven years later, California's Long Beach Unified School District required uniforms for all its schools. People claimed that school uniforms reduced violence and improved learning **environments**.

SCHOOL DRESS RULES: YEA OR NAY?

In a "Teens and Freedom" poll, more than 200,000 students were asked about school clothing rules.

Rule	Percentage in Favor
No gang symbols on clothing	75
No nose, lip, tongue, or eyebrow piercings	40
No bare stomachs	40
No short skirts	33
No baggy clothes	19
Uniforms	17

Information is from *USA Weekend*, "Teens and Freedom Survey Results," 2008.

DRESS FOR SUCCESS How can clothes improve schools? Many people believe that revealing clothes, like tank tops and low-rider pants, distract students from learning. Other people say sloppy sweat suits and extra-baggy clothes show disrespect. These people also think some clothing and symbols encourage gangs or cliques—tight circles of friends that keep other people out. Items such as bandannas, hoods, neck chains, and sunglasses can reflect gang **culture.** They can threaten violence, as if saying, "Watch out for us." Therefore, schools have banned clothes that might be linked with gangs or that might encourage drug or alcohol use or racism.

Schools that require students to wear uniforms say the rule has had positive effects. In the Long Beach schools, crime dropped by 76 percent. The schools also saw higher attendance. With greater safety and attendance, the schools say, learning increases. Uniforms may also increase school pride, bringing together students with **cultural** differences. Uniforms can also keep students from being divided into those who can afford trendy clothes and those who cannot. Neat, tasteful clothes may be less distracting and more respectful. They can send a different signal, one that says education is worthwhile.

FREE TO BE ME Not everyone believes that dress codes are good for students, however. Some people think such rules deny students' right to express themselves. Many students want freedom to show their differences. They do not think schools should ever discourage **diversity.** In some places, students and parents have brought lawsuits against schools with dress requirements. Those against dress codes also say that it is hard to prove rules about clothing improve schools.

Students and schools *do* usually agree that some rules for dress are necessary. However, many disagree about what those rules should be. The chart on the previous page shows students' feelings on dress restrictions. Most said they did not want uniforms. Tori, a student from Pennsylvania, put it this way: "I can sort of understand dress codes but not uniforms. Uniforms just take away **individuality,** [but] dress codes can help prevent some obvious signs of danger."

As schools decide on rules about student dress, they are considering more than skirt lengths and symbols on shirts. They hope to balance the rights of **individuals** with the safety and success of the school community. Now you "try on" the issue. Which side fits you best?

WRAP IT UP

Find It on the Page

1. What kinds of clothes are banned in many schools?

2. List three reasons why some people support dress codes.

3. Summarize why some people are against dress codes.

Use Clues

4. How might certain kinds of clothing encourage violence?

5. How—and why—would you change the dress code in your school?

6. Which is better—a strict dress code or school uniforms? Explain your answer.

Connect to the Big Question

After reading the article, do you think individual expression is more important than following a dress code? Explain.

Real-Life Connection

What do you know about the science of changing the weather? Find out by deciding if the statements below are true or false.

1. Humans can prevent tornadoes and hurricanes.
2. Scientists agree that adding chemicals to clouds can cause rain.
3. There are few reasons to spend money to change the weather.
4. Controlling weather could be dangerous and unfair.

Check It Out

Weather modification is the changing of weather artificially. Scientists hope to develop methods of weakening deadly storms and easing long dry spells, or droughts. They also hope to halt global warming, a rise in temperatures around the world. Meteorologists, people who study weather, work with other scientists to help farmers and firms that produce hydroelectric power, electricity made from the energy of running water.

WORD BANK

common (KAH muhn) *adjective*   Something that is **common** is ordinary or easily found.
EXAMPLE: *Tornadoes are **common** in the U.S. Midwest.*

community (kuh MYOO nuh tee) *noun*   A **community** is a group of people who live or work in the same area or who have similarities.
EXAMPLE: *The principal spoke to the student **community** on the first day of school.*

duty (DOO tee) *noun*   A **duty** is an action or way of behaving that is required by a person's job or sense of what is right.
EXAMPLE: *A teacher's **duty** is to set a good example for pupils.*

team (teem) *noun*   A **team** is a group of people who work towards a shared goal.
EXAMPLE: *Our football **team** may win most of its games this season.*

voice (voys) *verb*   When people **voice** their opinions, they speak their mind.
EXAMPLE: *How would you **voice** your concern about crime?*

Community or individual—which is more important?

Weather can strike with deadly force. It can ruin property, destroy crops, and kill people. However, weather can also be life-giving, bringing sorely needed rain. Changing the weather could be both helpful and harmful. As you read the article, ask yourself: Should we try to control the weather or let nature take its course?

Commanding the Weather

If you could control the weather, would you?

Imagine that satellites could zap tornadoes to weaken them. Suppose we could inject clouds with chemicals to produce rain. What if we could spread something on the sea to halt a hurricane? Those ideas may sound like fantasies. In fact, they are the focus of real projects that experts in weather modification are working on.

Altering weather could have huge benefits, but it could also create terrible problems. Weather disasters are far too **common.** They take thousands of lives each year and ring up billions of dollars in damage. If we could prevent such destruction, should we? Some people worry about the consequences of weather modification. Meteorologists and other scientists find that changing the weather poses complex questions.

CHANGES IN THE WIND The desire to control the weather is not new. Native peoples danced to make it rain. Modern weather modification began in 1946, when a scientist dropped dry ice from an airplane into a cloud. This "cloud seeding" started a snow flurry.

Today, cloud seeding is done with other chemicals as well. Scientists found that silver iodide attracts water in clouds and freezes it. The ice then falls to the earth as snow or (if it melts) rain. Silver iodide can be scattered from planes or shot into clouds. Seeding may result in an estimated 5 to 15 percent increase in rain or snow.

Cloud seeding is big business. Farmers purchase the service to ensure well-watered crops. States, cities, and hydroelectric power companies have spent millions on it. China leads the way, with a government weather modification program that costs $60 to $90 million a year. China also hopes to restrain the rain. Officials there promised dry weather for the opening of the 2008 Beijing Olympics.

Scientists are working on other kinds of weather modification, too. They believe that coating the ocean's surface with vegetable oil might weaken a hurricane. **Teams** of scientists are beaming microwave energy from satellites to try to stop tornadoes from developing. Other scientists are testing methods to guide the path of lightning. Researchers are even studying the possibility of using giant space mirrors to turn aside the sun's rays and reduce global warming.

A CONTROVERSIAL ISSUE People **voice** many reasons to pursue weather modification. It could help meet the growing need for water in overpopulated India and China. It might also reduce the costs of severe weather. U.S. droughts in the 1980s took more than 15,000 lives and cost $110 billion. If Hurricane Katrina—**commonly** thought to be the worst natural disaster in U.S. history—had been prevented, more than 1,000 lives might have been saved as well as an estimated $100 billion. Despite these possible benefits, weather modification is a hot topic. The scientific **community** cannot agree about its effectiveness.

U.S. WEATHER DESTRUCTION, 2006

The chart below shows the high cost of certain types of weather disasters in the United States in just one year.

Weather Event	People Killed	People Injured	Damage (in millions)
Lightning	47	246	$63.8
Tornadoes	67	989	$758.5
Hail	0	18	$1, 433.5
Floods	76	23	$118,850.5
Winter storms	17	109	$568.7
Drought	0	4	$2,636.1
High winds	26	133	$210.2
Total	233	1,522	$124,521.3

Information is from National Weather Service Office of Climate, Water, and Weather Services; National Climatic Data Center.

Studies cannot prove that seeded clouds would not have sent rain or snow anyway. Furthermore, scientists are concerned about toxic chemicals dropping from seeded clouds.

Then there is the fairness factor: What if making rain in Indiana means Ohio gets none? Is that "stealing" rain? A coastal farmer may need rain for crops, but the rain could hurt business at beach resorts. Who chooses? If we turn aside a hurricane from the United States but it spins destruction across Central America, are we responsible?

One Harvard University scientist explained the issue this way: "Let's say you have a mirror in space. Think of two summers ago when we were having this awful cold summer and Europe was having this awful heat wave. Who gets to adjust the mirror?"

Finally, could weather become a weapon? During the Vietnam War, U.S. planes seeded clouds over enemy supply roads, making them muddy and hard to use. The international **community** demanded and **dutifully** signed a treaty banning the use of weather modification for hostile purposes.

Interest in weather modification is unlikely to disappear. In 2007, Colorado congressman Mark Udall introduced a bill to fund its research. As scientists advance weather modification, however, they will have a **duty** to answer the complicated questions it raises.

WRAP IT UP

Find It on the Page

1. How are clouds seeded?

2. List three ways that weather modification could be helpful.

3. Summarize the arguments against weather modification.

Use Clues

4. Why does an international treaty ban weather modification for hostile purposes?

5. If weather modification was in use, what might three effects be?

6. If you controlled the weather, how would you decide whose interests should be served?

Connect to the Big Question

After reading the article, do you think we should try to control the weather, or should we let nature take its course?

Real–Life Connection
Can you predict what this article will be about? Read the title and headings in the chart. Then use them to predict the content of the article. Write your predictions on your own paper.

Title and Headings	Prediction
Title: Restoring Cities from the Ground Up	
Heading 1: Clean It Up!	
Heading 2: Grow a Garden—and More!	
Heading 3: Lasting Effects?	

custom (KUHS tuhm) *noun*   A **custom** is an action or habit done regularly.
EXAMPLE: *It is a **custom** to give people gifts on their birthday.*

ethnicity (eth NI suh tee) *noun*   Your **ethnicity** is the background, culture, traditions, language, and nationality you share with similar people.
EXAMPLE: *My family came to the United States from Mexico, so we enjoy music that celebrates our Mexican-American **ethnicity**.*

group (groop) *noun*   A **group** is a number of individuals who have things in common, such as family, community, work, or interests.
EXAMPLE: *My friends and I formed a study **group** to help us prepare for tests.*

unify (YOO nuh fy) *verb*   To **unify** people is to bring them together.
EXAMPLE: *When disaster strikes, people **unify** their efforts to help others who are affected.*

various (VER ee uhs) *adjective*   When you have **various** things or ideas, you have different kinds.
EXAMPLE: *Harriet's vegetable soup is made of **various** vegetables, including potatoes, beans, corn, and carrots.*

Community or individual—which is more important?

Unfortunately, many urban areas are plagued by poverty, violence, and decay. Youths and other citizens are working to clean up their communities. In some cities, they are building beautiful gardens to bring people together. As you read the article, ask yourself: **Can an urban garden really help turn a community around?**

Restoring Cities from the Ground Up

James Stanley owns an auto body shop in Philadelphia. Ten years ago, he began planting gardens in Philly's vacant lots. What does a body shop have to do with turning lots into gardens? Both are about second chances, and so is Stanley. He urges neighborhood youths, many with troubles, to come work in a **group** and learn in his gardens.

James Stanley is not the only person who thinks a patch of green in the city is a good idea. People all around the country are trying to restore their communities. They believe that cleanup days, tree-planting projects, or city vegetable gardens can help.

CLEAN IT UP! Why do urban communities become run-down and dangerous? They can get this way when people feel powerless to change their situations. Many individuals and **groups** are trying to turn that helplessness around. In Pittsburgh, an organization called Teens Against Senseless Violence (TASK) is showing young people how to take ownership of their neighborhood and make a difference.

Planting gardens in abandoned lots is one way to help turn around a community. ▶

The leader of TASK, Mikhail Pappas, started a project called Luv Ur Block. This project works to **unify** teens to clean up litter in their neighborhood. As a result, they are learning to lead their community in a positive direction.

Young people in Albany, New York, also found that **unification** could help improve their city. University of Albany students and local Boy Scout troops worked side by side on Albany's Make a Difference Day. Volunteers picked up garbage, swept sidewalks, and pulled weeds. Many Boy Scouts had a personal interest in the project. They took new pride in the places where they lived because of the project. A fourteen-year-old who took part in the project explained, "These are our streets we're cleaning." The Make a Difference Day in Albany has now become a yearly **custom.**

It is possible to learn many skills by working in a community garden.

GROW A GARDEN—AND MORE! Some cities are taking community cleanup to the next level. They want their neighborhoods to blossom and thrive. Urban gardeners are turning abandoned areas into beautiful oases of flowers, vegetables, trees, and more. In Washington, D.C., the Urban Garden Development Program knew it had to deal with a filthy, rat-infested backyard at the Latin American Youth Center's Transitional Living Program. To tackle the problem, project organizers gathered fifty local youths. Together, the organizers and the neighborhood young people planned and constructed a lush garden with a basketball court and a picnic area. In just one year, the project was complete.

City Farm is another urban garden that has improved a community. City Farm is an organic vegetable farm located between two Chicago neighborhoods. The farm grows **various** vegetables and sells them to the public and to restaurants. City Farm provides jobs, farming education, and affordable nutrition to the community.

LASTING EFFECTS? Can gardens really change communities? Some people do not believe that urban cleanup and gardening can have long-lasting effects. These people wonder if enthusiasm for such projects will wane and if other efforts would be more worthwhile. They believe communities might be made stronger by building low-cost housing on empty lots. Some people look at a vacant city lot and see only income possibility. They say many garden plots belong to the cities themselves. The cities lost taxes when the lots were wastelands. If developers bought the parcels and built businesses there, the taxes those businesses would pay could help the communities financially.

However, people who organize community cleanups and urban gardens believe that community members are gaining a **variety** of valuable skills. Once **unaccustomed** to gardening, young people become handy with tools and learn to grow food. Kids do research, raise money, and develop lasting values. Bridging differences between people, no matter what their **ethnicity,** creates neighborhood **unity.** In the process, community members cultivate a real sense of belonging. New skills, knowledge, and values can empower young people to overcome future challenges and set new goals. That is the thing about empowerment: It grows, just like a garden.

WRAP IT UP

Find It on the Page

1. What are two goals of the Luv Ur Block project?

2. Name one result of Albany's Make a Difference Day.

3. List three ways working in an urban garden can benefit young people.

Use Clues

4. Why might some people be against planting urban gardens?

5. How could you use the information in this article to improve your community?

6. What benefits do all the projects mentioned in the article have in common?

Connect to the Big Question

After reading the article, do you think an urban garden can really help turn around a community?

Real-Life Connection

Imagine you are on a soccer team. To celebrate a big win, your team plans a night out. Suddenly, your team captain tells all of you that a teammate broke her leg and is recovering at home. Your captain plans to visit her instead of going on the outing. She would like you all to do the same but wants each member to decide. What do you think of the team leader's decision? What would you do? Write your ideas on a chart like this one.

What I think of the team leader's decision:	Why?
What I would do:	Why?

WORD BANK

duty (DOO tee) *noun*   A **duty** is an action or way of behaving that is required by a person's job or sense of what is right.
   EXAMPLE: *It is the **duty** of police officers to enforce the law and protect people from harm.*

individual (in duh VIJ wuhl) *noun*   An **individual** is one person.
   EXAMPLE: *Every **individual** in our family has a unique set of interests.*

team (teem) *noun*   A **team** is a group of people who work toward a shared goal.
   EXAMPLE: *I am a member of my club's leadership **team,** which meets every Wednesday after school.*

tradition (truh DI shuhn) *noun*   A meaningful belief or habit passed down over time is a **tradition.**
   EXAMPLE: *It is a **tradition** in my family to eat sweet-potato pie and stuffing on Thanksgiving.*

THE BIG ?

Community or individual—which is more important?

What makes a person a good leader? Is it intelligence, talent, a charming personality? Successful leaders usually have the ability to accomplish important goals, to earn the respect of the people they direct, and to inspire other people. How do they excel? As you read the article, ask yourself: What makes a good leader?

What It Takes to Lead

You see them on TV and read about them. They are heads of countries, companies, schools, and **teams.** They serve in powerful positions, motivate people, and solve problems. They are our best leaders. What does leadership really mean, though? Scholars have studied successful presidents, managers, teachers, and chiefs. The scholars can pinpoint traits that set these leaders apart. What makes a superior leader is often a combination of positive qualities.

THREE WHO LEAD Mike Krzyzewski (shuh SHEF skee) is Duke University's head basketball coach. Krzyzewski has had many achievements. He is a twelve-time National Coach of the Year. His **teams** have played in National Collegiate Athletic Association (NCAA) tournaments twenty-three times and won three championships. He has led nineteen All-American players. Player of the Year Jason Williams admires Coach Krzyzewski. "I'd run through a brick wall for him," Williams once said.

Coach Mike Krzyzewski works with one of his players.

Krzyzewski inspires devotion because he values his **team** above everything else. He gives his players and staff credit for Duke's impressive basketball **tradition.** He emphasizes **teamwork** above the **individual.** "It's not his way or her way," he tells players. "It's *our* way."

THE WAY TO SAFETY Captain Jay Jonas is a New York City firefighter. On September 11, 2001, he did the almost unthinkable thing: He ran into a burning building, not out of it. After terrorists flew airplanes into the World Trade Center, thousands of people were trapped in the fiery Twin Towers. Jonas's **duty** was to help them.

> Coach Krzyzewski says, "It's not his way or her way. It's *our* way."

Carrying heavy equipment, Jonas and his **team** climbed the north tower stairs. As they reached the twenty-eighth floor, the building started to shake violently. Jonas ordered his **team** to evacuate. As he and the other firefighters descended, they discovered Josephine, an older woman who was too exhausted to go on. Helping her would slow their escape, but they refused to abandon her. Then the tower fell. Amazingly, the stairwell Jonas and his **team** were on held. They spent hours in darkness, encouraging Josephine, until rescuers helped them and her to safety. Their survival seemed like a miracle. They all could have died, like 343 other firefighters that day.

STORIES THAT MATTER Lisa Ling is one of the United States' top TV news journalists. Known for her fearless sense of adventure, she reports from some of the world's most dangerous places. Ling began her career at age sixteen, as the host of a news show for teens. Soon she was reporting for the national school TV network Channel One News. As a war correspondent, she went undercover to remote and war-torn countries, including Colombia, Afghanistan, Iraq, and Iran.

Ling went on to work for other news groups and to host the National Geographic Channel's *Explorer* program. Throughout her career, she has investigated terrorists, drug wars, and urban gangs. She has faced many dangers, and her work has often exposed injustices. Interviewing refugees, victims of abuse, and other people whose stories often go unheard, Lisa Ling has given voice to many who suffer.

PUTTING OTHERS FIRST What qualities do these three leaders share? Each of them puts other people first. Coach Krzyzewski gives his players and staff the credit for his **team's** success. Jay Jonas puts others' safety before his own. Lisa Ling takes on dangerous assignments to share with the world other people's important stories. The three leaders all show an important trait of good leaders: selflessness, or the willingness to make personal sacrifices.

With an attitude of humility, they empower others to become leaders themselves. Mike Krzyzewski urges his players to serve their communities in social projects, including education, cancer research, and health care for children. In doing so, he supports his players' preparation for leadership. Jay Jonas shows by example what a **dutiful** public servant must do. Lisa Ling is a role model for those who work to make a difference. To encourage young leaders, she hosted a TV program featuring "20 Teens Who Will Change the World."

Leaders have to have the right qualities: dedication, commitment to excellence, a sense of fairness, courage, and compassion. Through their selfless accomplishments, they earn the respect of their communities and even the world.

WRAP IT UP

Find It on the Page

1. What does it mean for a leader to be selfless?

2. Compare and contrast the ways that Mike Krzyzewski and Jay Jonas are selfless.

3. Summarize the way Lisa Ling shows leadership.

Use Clues

4. What effect can selfless leaders have on teams?

5. Think of other leaders you know. How do they exhibit some of the qualities mentioned in this article?

6. What aspects or experiences of your own life might prepare you to be a leader?

Connect to the Big Question

After reading the article, what do you think makes a good leader?

Real-Life Connection

What do you know about the ways communities solve problems that natural disasters can cause? Rate your knowledge on a chart like this one:

Type of Disaster	Know a Lot	Know a Little	Know Nothing
Tornado			
Flood			
Wildfire			

Check It Out

Certain parts of the United States are more likely to experience disasters. Greensburg, Kansas, is right in "tornado alley," a wide swath of the Midwest where tornadoes often occur. New Orleans had a levee system that some experts knew could not protect the city from the most severe hurricanes. Southern California is prey every year to hot Santa Ana winds, which can turn fires into infernos.

community (kuh MYOO nuh tee) *noun*   A **community** is a group of people who live or work in the same area or who have similarities.
EXAMPLE: *Our **community** of students, parents, and teachers puts on a fall festival every October.*

culture (KUHL chuhr) *noun*   A **culture** is the set of beliefs and habits that form a way of life for a group of people.
EXAMPLE: *I enjoy the music and food of Middle Eastern **culture.***

family (FAM lee) *noun*   A **family** is a group of people related by common ancestry.
EXAMPLE: *I have a brother and a sister in my **family.***

persuade (puhr SWAYD) *verb*   When you **persuade** people, you convince them to do or believe something.
EXAMPLE: *Alex is trying to **persuade** me to try out for the team.*

unify (YOO nuh fy) *verb*   To **unify** people is to bring them together.
EXAMPLE: *The hurricane caused a lot of damage, but it did **unify** neighbors in an effort to rebuild.*

Community or individual—which is more important?

Terrible though they can be, the worst events sometimes bring out the best in people. Natural disasters, such as tornadoes, hurricanes, and wildfires, occur every year in the United States. When disaster strikes, communities usually unite to recover. As you read the article, ask yourself: **What does it take to make a community unite and rebuild?**

Rebuilding Communities

Have you ever heard a tornado roar overhead? Have you ever clung to a roof while floodwaters surged? Have you ever fled the furious flames of wildfires? If you have been through a natural disaster, you know how devastating it can be. Besides simply surviving, victims face other difficulties. Disasters separate people from loved ones, cause injury and death, and destroy homes and businesses. Some people lose everything.

Recent disasters in the United States have posed overwhelming challenges to relief efforts. These efforts tend to **unify** the people in a **community,** requiring them to work together to ease suffering and to recover. What problems do the people face, and how do they band together?

▲ **Hurricane Katrina destroyed this home.**

IN THE FACE OF DISASTER In May 2007, a massive tornado struck the town of Greensburg, Kansas, destroying 95 percent of the small farming **community.** The 205-mile-per-hour winds leveled more than 900 homes and many churches. Nine people died. Stunned survivors were left without schools, water, power, or passable roads. With a hundred businesses gone, people lost their jobs. Some people with **family** nearby simply moved.

The New Orleans, Louisiana, area experienced what many people call the worst natural disaster in U.S. history when Hurricane Katrina hit in August 2005. Storm waters surged 19 feet above sea level, completely demolishing homes and ruining **communities.** Streets turned to rivers filled with poisons, threatening disease. Thousands of people were forced into temporary shelters with nothing but what they carried. Government relief aid seemed to take a long time: first days, then weeks, then months. One year later, hundreds of Katrina victims taken to cities like Austin, Texas, were still waiting to go home.

Recovering from a disaster requires a community effort.

Thousands of people from Southern California also had to flee their homes when wildfires caused devastation. In 2003, fires took more than twenty lives in twenty-two **communities.** In 2007, the Santa Ana winds whipped up fires again, leaving fourteen people dead and nearly a hundred injured. Half a million acres were burned. In both years, thousands of houses were destroyed. Long after the fires were put out, many victims were still waiting for insurance settlements. New government rules in some areas made reconstruction harder.

WHAT COMMUNITIES CAN DO Despite hardships after a disaster, **communities** somehow find ways to go on. Instead of letting the hardships tear them apart, people **unite** to move forward. The need to rebuild is not the only thing that **unifies** people after a disaster strikes. Kind assistance, emotional support, and a spirit of hope also link these people to one another.

Greensburg residents are bound by a determination to keep their town alive. A man who lost his home explains: "There's going to be [people from my family] in this county for a long time. We've been through droughts and blizzards. This is another complication in the road." Town leaders were able to **persuade** citizens that the disaster could be an opportunity to create a cutting-edge Greensburg. They are researching ways to build an environmentally friendly town that uses less energy than before. They hope to build a wind energy plant and produce alternative fuel from corn. Their optimism is contagious and serves to ignite the **community's** will to recover.

Despite the distance from their home, Katrina survivors in Austin have kept their **communities** alive by celebrating their **culture.** They created a gathering called Celebration Restore Our Citizens of Katrina. **Cultural** events included jazz music and Creole food.

California fire victims have not given up, either. People formed rebuilding organizations to provide support, such as the San Diego Firestorm **Community** Recovery Team. They share information, establish project funds, and hire professionals.

Experts say that **communities** can cope with disasters by focusing on the big picture, not on individual losses. Finding ways to help neighbors in need connects people, as does a willingness to listen, comfort, share faith, and show **community** pride. California governor Arnold Schwarzenegger sums up the attitude this way: "I know we can do this. We are resolute in our spirit. We are determined to rebuild. We are, after all, Californians."

WRAP IT UP

Find It on the Page

1. What problems did the tornado create for Greensburg residents?

2. How have New Orleans citizens in Austin, Texas, kept their communities alive from afar?

3. What are four or more qualities that bring communities together in times of hardship?

Use Clues

4. Why would creating a new kind of town help unite Greensburg?

5. If a fire, hurricane, or tornado struck a community in your state, how would you help the community recover?

6. What similar challenges were faced by each of the disaster areas mentioned in the article?

Connect to the Big Question

After reading the article, what do you think it takes to make a community unite and rebuild?

Real-Life Connection

Why do people like to share crazy stories, even when the stories are untrue? Use a word web like the one below to jot down your ideas.

People share stories because . . .

Check It Out

Urban myths are fictional stories that are shared among many people and told as if they were true. Urban myths caution about dangers or teach a lesson. They can be funny, shocking, embarrassing, or have a combination of qualities. Urban myths are often spread by word of mouth or by e-mail.

WORD BANK

common (KAH muhn) *adjective*   Something that is **common** is ordinary or easily found.
EXAMPLE: *Colds are **common** illnesses during the winter.*

group (groop) *noun*   A **group** is a number of individuals who have things in common, such as family, community, work, or interests.
EXAMPLE: *A **group** of volunteers will help us decorate for the dance.*

tradition (truh DI shuhn) *noun*   A meaningful belief or habit passed down over time is a **tradition.**
EXAMPLE: *Attending a baseball game each spring is a **tradition** in my family.*

unique (yoo NEEK) *verb*   If something is **unique,** it is one of a kind.
EXAMPLE: *Each handmade work of art is **unique.***

Community or individual—which is more important?

Have you heard a crazy story from a friend or read one on e-mail that made you laugh out loud or frightened you? Such stories may be urban myths. They spread like rumors, passed by people who are not really sure if the stories are true. As you read the article, ask yourself: What purposes do urban myths serve?

The Irresistible Urban Myth

Have you heard about the girl who found a cockroach in her taco? How about the kid who discovered an alligator in the washroom? Do you think those stories are true? Even if they are not, would you share them with others? Many people find it irresistible to pass along stories called urban myths.

Stories like urban myths have probably existed for as long as people have communicated. Fairy tales with scary forests and dragons, even bogeyman and campfire stories, are forerunners of urban myths. Relating them today has become a **tradition** in many cultures.

Urban myths come in many forms. Some reflect the **common** fears and concerns of the time, and some are simply entertaining. Other myths make people cringe in shock or sigh in sympathy.

CAUTIONARY TALES One popular kind of urban myth is the cautionary tale, which warns people about potential dangers.

Many urban myths are passed along by word of mouth.

Food contamination is a popular subject in cautionary tales. Examples include bugs crawling through packaged foods and a rat lying in a bucket of fried chicken!

Frightening events are also **commonly** found in cautionary tales. Do you know the story about the man who awakened in a hotel bathtub full of ice? Freezing and confused, the man noticed a note taped to the phone. It instructed him to call the police. When officers rushed him to the hospital, doctors discovered that one of his kidneys had been removed. The last thing the man remembered was flirting with a beautiful woman. The police said criminals were stealing organs and selling them. This story cautions people to think twice before flirting with strangers!

Many urban myths are frightening.

SHOCK VALUE AND SYMPATHY SCAMS Some urban myths are just plain shocking, and people share them to see other people squirm. Maybe it is a cultural phenomenon. After all, people produce hundreds of horror films each year to provoke a similar response.

Many people pass along outrageous tales just to see how far they can push a hoax. Such pranks give the storytellers a thrill.

Another type of urban myth is the sympathy scam. You get an e-mail story about a sick child, and it pulls your heartstrings. If you forward the story to a hundred people, the ploy promises, a few pennies for each will go to a foundation to cure the child's disease. Perhaps sharing such stories makes people feel selfless and giving.

JUST FOR LAUGHS? Funny stories fill another **group** of **traditional** urban myths. Did you hear about the screaming woman who was parked in her car at a grocery store? When a bystander hurried to her aid, the woman shrieked, "I've been shot!" She was clutching a gooey substance at the back of her head, but upon closer inspection, the bystander realized that the goo was not brains. It was biscuit dough!

A can of biscuit dough had exploded in the back seat. The woman had been hit with little more than a scare. The joy of making others laugh is one reason that people repeat urban myths. Circulating such stories has snicker appeal. It is almost like gossiping, but it does not hurt anyone.

Even if an urban myth started with a shred of truth, it soon bears little similarity to the original tale, because people add their own **unique** details. Each version becomes subjective, colored by the teller's viewpoint. Thus, people repeat urban myths for another reason: to practice their storytelling art. Stories connect individuals with a community. Each teller gains an audience and perhaps even status as the relayer of "information."

Why do people believe urban myths? Many of the stories contain credible details, like real locations and activities. Most, however, are not backed by evidence. Many of these stories are told to us by friends we trust. Likewise, many stories on the Internet smack of truth. Still, as author Leo Rosten once wrote, "I never cease being dumbfounded by the unbelievable things people believe." Before you take a story as true, use your judgment. If the story seems too bizarre, too vague, or too good to be true, it probably is. Why do you think people call them "myths"?

WRAP IT UP

Find It on the Page

1. What are four forms that urban myths can take?

2. What is a cautionary tale?

3. Why do people share urban myths? Give three reasons.

Use Clues

4. Why might people repeat stories without checking to see if the stories are true?

5. What urban myths, if any, have you passed along, and why have you done so?

6. Which do you think is worse—gossiping or passing along an urban myth? Why?

Connect to the Big Question

Now that you have read the article, what purposes do you think urban myths serve?

Real-Life Connection

Your school has just started a community-service program. What would you do to pitch in? In a chart like the one below, write down how one person could make a difference by volunteering for each activity.

Type of Volunteer Work or Project	How Could One Person Make a Difference?
Assist sick or elderly people	
Tutor struggling students	
Restore a habitat or home	
Work in a soup kitchen	
Clean up the environment	

WORD BANK

completely (kuhm PLEET lee) *adverb*   If you do something **completely,** you do it fully or bring an end to it.
EXAMPLE: *Make sure the cookies are **completely** baked before removing them from the oven.*

diversity (duh VUHR suh tee) *noun*   If a group has **diversity,** it is made of many different kinds of people or things.
EXAMPLE: *That college's student body has broad **diversity,** including people from many backgrounds.*

environment (in VY ruhn muhnt) *noun*   Your **environment** is made up of your surroundings.
EXAMPLE: *My **environment** is my city neighborhood.*

ethnicity (eth NI suh tee) *noun*   Your **ethnicity** is the background, culture, traditions, language, and nationality you share with similar people.
EXAMPLE: *During Black History Month, people focus on learning about the history of those with African American **ethnicity**.*

individual (in duh VIJ wuhl) *noun*   An **individual** is one person.
EXAMPLE: *If every **individual** would spend time volunteering, people could make a big difference in their communities.*

Community or individual—which is more important?

What can you do about world problems? Do you wish you could change things? Do you feel like such a little drop in a bucket that nothing can happen till all the other drops get busy? As you read the article, ask yourself: Do small, individual efforts really matter, or must large, group efforts be made for real change to occur?

The Ripple Effect

Look around. Do you ever feel **completely** overwhelmed by troubles you see in your community? Violence, discrimination, trash, waste, poverty, disease, hunger—you name it. Some problems might seem too big to fix. Maybe you think that to make changes, you need to have a lot of money or to join with millions of other people. Maybe you feel that there is not much one person can do.

If so, go pitch a rock into a pond and watch what happens. No matter how small the rock is, ripples of water will radiate outward from the place where it hit the water. That is called the "ripple effect," and it happens when many things flow from one small action.

Some people believe that the ripple effect can change the world: One person with a good idea affects the life of another, then other people notice, and suddenly more people begin using that idea to help others. In this way, one **individual** becomes a force for real change. "All great things start with one person," people say. Others claim, "It takes a village." What do you think?

TEENS FOR HUMANITY Jennica Jenkins is a "ripple" person. As a counselor at California's Moorpark High, she dealt with students facing all kinds of problems.

Jennifer Staple is just one person who started a "ripple effect." ▶

Their problems included drug and alcohol use, racial discrimination, and physical and emotional abuse. She feared that students' difficulties would carry over into adulthood. How could she stop the cycle?

Jenkins had an idea: What if all students, regardless of **ethnicity,** had a place where they felt they belonged and a way to connect and create healthy, respectful relationships? What if they learned to talk about problems instead of using violence? What if they had resources to help prevent risky behaviors?

From Jenkins's idea, Teens for Humanity (TFH) was born. TFH is an organization that has grown to include 300 students at Moorpark High. Soon after TFH began, violence decreased at the school, and membership in support groups increased. Other schools noticed, and TFH expanded to more than 200 chapters countrywide.

TFH celebrates **diversity.** The organization is dedicated to bringing **diverse** students together to share experiences, create a supportive **environment,** diffuse violence, find assistance, and hold special events. At one chapter's "Peace on Campus Day," young people remember those who have been victims of violence. Another chapter's "Don't Be Stupid, Cupid" project raises awareness about dating violence.

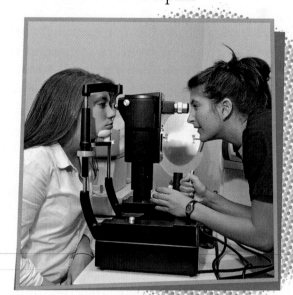

▲ **Unite for Sight offers eye exams like this one.**

Jenkins believes young people have the power to change the world. She sums up her support of them this way: "Teenagers are not the problem. They are the solution."

UNITE FOR SIGHT Jennifer Staple is another example of how one young person's idea can change the world. Staple was between her first two years of college when she took a summer job at an eye doctor's office. She was saddened by how many people had lost their sight from preventable diseases. She decided to do something about the problem.

In 2000, Staple created an organization to bring free eye screening and education to people in need. Unite for Sight began with just a few volunteers at her school, Yale University. Students were trained to do simple eye screenings and to match patients with volunteer doctors and programs to pay for treatment. There was such an enthusiastic response that Staple expanded the program into surrounding New Haven, Connecticut. Now the program has 400,000 volunteers in ninety chapters around the world. By the end of 2007, Unite for Sight had provided about 12,000 sight-restoring surgeries and countless treatments for eye diseases.

A CHAIN REACTION Expressing determination and **individuality,** Jenkins and Staple assisted many people with their programs. Their efforts involved many other people, all coming together to form a chain reaction of change. Think of this: A chain reaction has to start somewhere, right? The action of just one **individual** can set off that reaction, like a rock setting off ripples in a pond. You never know how far those ripples might go.

WRAP IT UP

Find It on the Page

1. What is Teens for Humanity dedicated to doing?

2. What made Jennifer Staple create Unite for Sight?

3. Briefly explain how the ripple effect involves people trying to make a difference in the world.

Use Clues

4. In your opinion, why have so many schools started TFH chapters?

5. What can you learn from Jennifer Staple about accomplishing change?

6. How are the Teens for Humanity and Unite for Sight programs similar?

Connect to the Big Question

Now that you have read the article, do you think small efforts that individuals make really matter, or can change happen only when many people work together? Explain.

Real-Life Connection

What do you know about tricksters? Find out by telling whether you agree or disagree with each statement below.

1. A trickster is always a villain, or bad guy, in a story.
2. People often find tricksters funny.
3. A trickster usually plays by the rules.
4. As story characters, tricksters are popular with readers.

Check It Out

A trickster is an amusing character who seeks and finds trouble, disobeys rules, plays pranks, and frequently fools others. The trickster usually gets away with bad behavior without the punishment one would find in the real world. Tricksters appear in folktales, myths, children's stories, cartoons, movies, novels, and more.

WORD BANK

argue (AHR gyoo) *verb*　When you **argue,** you give reasons for or against an idea.
EXAMPLE: *The student council will **argue** against changing the date for the senior prom.*

culture (KUHL chuhr) *noun*　A **culture** is the set of beliefs and habits that form a way of life for a group of people.
EXAMPLE: *Freedom and individuality are important values in U.S. **culture.***

custom (KUHS tuhm) *noun*　A **custom** is an action or habit done regularly.
EXAMPLE: *In my family, it is a **custom** for my father to carve the Thanksgiving turkey.*

family (FAM lee) *noun*　A **family** is a group of people related by common ancestry.
EXAMPLE: *My mother's **family** is related to the Pilgrims who landed at Plymouth Rock.*

unique (yoo NEEK) *verb*　If something is **unique,** it is one of a kind.
EXAMPLE: *Every snowflake is **unique.***

Community or individual—which is more important?

Stop following the rules and you will probably wind up in trouble. A trickster, however, will not. Tricksters can charm their way out of any situation. We admire them and laugh at their pranks. In fact, some of our most beloved television and movie characters are tricksters. As you read the article, ask yourself: **What makes trickster characters so appealing?**

TRICKSTER APPEAL REVEALED!

Y ou know that kid in class who makes trouble, makes you laugh, and even makes you like him—the one who always gets away with everything? Believe it or not, he is a modern-day trickster. As a character, Trickster is as old as the hills and as young as you are. Where did Trickster come from?

Tricksters have been around for as long as storytelling itself. Bad and bold yet likable, these characters have roots in myths and folklore. Br'er Rabbit is one. He is called Brother Rabbit in African **cultures.** Bugs Bunny is another. He is related to Nanabozho, a Native American figure. Tricksters are not just rabbits, though. They include coyotes, spiders, turtles, foxes, and humans. Tricksters get themselves into all kinds of jams, and we love them for it.

TRICKY, SLICK, AND SLY Remember that U.S. cartoon character Wile E. Coyote? He is forever trying to catch Roadrunner with traps, bombs, and other crazy devices. Despite sly planning, Coyote always ends up falling off a cliff or blowing himself up. His enemy, Roadrunner, just speeds away with a "Beep-beep!"

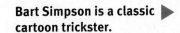

Bart Simpson is a classic cartoon trickster. ▶

Wile E. Coyote has many trickster characteristics. He can be mean and funny at the same time. Trying to snare Roadrunner, he causes many of his own problems. Tricksters make a mess for themselves and others by disobeying the rules. They do things most of us would not dare to do. Somehow, though, they always survive. With almost magical powers, they slide out of slippery situations by the skin of their teeth. Roadrunner himself is a bit of a trickster, as he frequently out-tricks Coyote.

> **Tricksters make a mess for themselves and others by disobeying the rules.**

Tricksters may seem less capable than others, but they always prove to be more clever. The tortoise in "The Tortoise and the Hare" is slower than the hare, but he outwits the hare to win the race.

BUGS, BART, AND CAPTAIN JACK The most famous cartoon trickster of all is Bugs Bunny, many people might **argue.** This clever rabbit has been outsmarting hunter Elmer Fudd since 1940. Despite Fudd's efforts to bag him, Bugs escapes in style by putting on funny disguises, throwing lit sticks of dynamite, or slipping down his rabbit hole. At the peak of Fudd's frustration, Bugs's **custom** is to respond, "Ehh, what's up, Doc?"

Bart Simpson is a popular modern cartoon trickster. The ten-year-old in the *Simpsons* TV **family,** Bart plays pranks and rebels against authority. His bad habits include using his armpit as a musical instrument. Question his poor behavior, and his **customary** response will be, "Don't have a cow, man!"

Captain Jack Sparrow, from the *Pirates of the Caribbean* movies, is a **unique** film trickster. Living by his own rules, he says and does whatever he likes. He switches sides when it suits him. He seeks treasure and fame and gets into scrapes and **arguments** with his enemies. Writer Terry Rossio says, "The fun thing about Jack . . . is that he's not particularly good at avoiding getting caught. He *will* get caught; you just can't hold on to him for very long." Both clumsy and slick, sassy Jack charms us with a flair that is common to tricksters.

WHAT IS THEIR APPEAL? Despite their schemes and scams, we applaud tricksters. Not only do they make us laugh, but they also appeal to the rebel in us. When tricksters break the rules by doing unexpected things, they also break our boredom. Their creativity and individuality encourage the same qualities in us. Their cleverness can inspire us to find clever solutions. Trickster characters may even help keep society from getting too restricted. They show that life does not always have to follow a set of rules. It can be fun and a little silly, too.

When a trickster misbehaves, part of us does want to see him or her get punished. Perhaps the punishment reassures us that order will prevail in a community or a **culture.** In the real world, bad behavior has consequences. Despite recognizing this, we also want to see that the trickster comes out OK.

We like the trickster and do not want to see too harsh a punishment. In a trickster's world, there is always a way out. When tricksters escape, we feel as if we escape with them. That might be why children cheer on tricksters: No matter how naughty tricksters are, they know they will always get a second chance.

WRAP IT UP

Find It on the Page

1. Where does the trickster tradition come from?

2. List four common traits of a trickster character.

3. Summarize why some people think Bugs Bunny and Captain Jack Sparrow are lovable characters.

Use Clues

4. According to the article, why do people admire tricksters?

5. How might trickster characters help society?

6. How might a trickster's antics cross the line?

Connect to the Big Question

After reading the article, what do you think makes trickster characters so appealing?"

 **Interview**

Answer the Big Question: Community or individual—which is more important?

You have read articles about communities and individuals. Use what you learned to answer the Unit 6 Big Question (BQ).

UNIT 6 ARTICLES

The Great Dress Debate,
pp. 168–171

Commanding the Weather,
pp. 172–175

Restoring Cities from the Ground Up,
pp. 176–179

What It Takes to Lead,
pp. 180–183

Rebuilding Communities,
pp. 184–187

The Irresistible Urban Myth,
pp. 188–191

The Ripple Effect,
pp. 192–195

Trickster Appeal Revealed!
pp. 196–199

STEP 1: Partner Up and Choose

Your first step is to pick Unit 6 articles that you like.

Get together. Find a partner to work with.

Read the list of articles. Discuss which articles listed on the left side of this page were the most interesting to you.

Choose two or more articles. Pick articles that you both agree on.

STEP 2: Reread and Answer the Unit Big Question

Your next step is to answer the Unit BQ with your partner.

Reread the articles you chose. As you reread, think about the Unit BQ.

Interview your partner. Ask these questions about each article:

- What issue is this article about? What does this article tell you about individuals or a community?
- How does the information in this article help you answer the Unit BQ: Community or individual—which is more important?

Take notes. As your partner answers the questions, take interview notes to record his or her responses.

STEP 3: Discuss and Give Reasons

During this step, talk with your partner about his or her answer to the Unit BQ.

Discuss the answer to the Unit BQ. Ask your partner to list reasons based on things he or she read in the articles:

- What details in the articles helped you pick your answer?
- Are there times when both individuals and communities are important?

Write your partner's answers. Add to your interview notes. Use another sheet of paper if you need to.

STEP 4: Add Examples

Now, finish the interview by asking for real-life examples.

Prompt your partner. To help your partner think even more deeply about the Unit BQ ask him or her for a real-life example:

- Which do you think is more important—the community or the individual? Why?
- Describe a time when you think that you or another individual in your community was more important than the community.

Add to your notes. Add your partner's example to the interview notes. Be sure your notes have specific details.

STEP 5: Check and Fix

Next, you and your partner will look over the interview notes to see whether they could be improved.

Use the rubric. Use the questions to evaluate your work. Answer each question yes or no. Then trade interview notes with your partner. Use the rubric to evaluate your partner's work.

Discuss your evaluations. Explain to your partner why you answered a question yes or no. For every no answer, explain what your partner could do to get a yes answer.

Improve your interview notes. If your interview notes could be improved, fix the mistakes or add more details.

STEP 6: Practice and Present

Get ready to present your partner's viewpoint to classmates.

Practice what you want to say. You will use your interview notes to explain how your partner answered the Unit BQ. Think about what you will need to say. Practice your presentation with your partner.

Present your interview notes. Introduce your partner to the class and explain how he or she answered the Unit 6 BQ. Include at least one specific example from an article and one from your partner's own experiences. Consider using a multimedia tool to summarize your main points for your audience.

GLOSSARY

This glossary will help you quickly find definitions of Word Bank words.

A

affect (uh FEKT) *verb* To **affect** something is to create a change in it.

analyze (A nuh lyz) *verb* When you **analyze** something, you divide it into parts and see how they fit together.

appearance (uh PIR uhns) *noun* The **appearance** of a situation, place, or thing is its outward look.

appreciate (uh PREE shee ayt) *verb* To **appreciate** something means to value it.

approach (uh PROHCH) *noun* An **approach** is an organized way to do something or to get somewhere.

argue (AHR gyoo) *verb* When you **argue,** you give reasons for or against an idea.

assume (uh SOOM) *verb* When you **assume** something, you suppose that it is true without checking to make sure.

assumption (uh SUHM shun) *noun* If you make an **assumption,** you suppose something is true without checking to make sure.

attitude (A tuh tood) *noun* Your **attitude** toward something is the way you think or feel about it.

awareness (uh WER nuhs) *noun* **Awareness** is knowing that something, such as a problem, exists.

B

background (BAK rownd) *noun* Your **background** is made up of your experiences, knowledge, and education.

believable (buh LEE vuh bul) *adjective* When something is **believable,** it seems possible or true.

bias (BY uhs) *noun* When you show a **bias,** you show a like or a dislike that prevents you from being fair.

C

challenge (CHA luhnj) *noun* A **challenge** is something that is difficult and takes extra effort to do.

characteristic (ker ik tuh RIS tik) *noun* A **characteristic** is a trait that describes a person or thing.

common (KAH muhn) *adjective* Something that is **common** is ordinary or easily found.

communicate (kuh MYOO nuh kayt) *verb* To **communicate** is to give or receive information.

communication (kuh myoo nuh KAY shuhn) *noun* **Communication** is the

factual (FAK chuh wuhl) *adjective* Something that is **factual** is real or true.

family (FAM lee) *noun* A **family** is a group of people related by common ancestry.

fiction (FIK shuhn) *noun* **Fiction** is writing or ideas that come from the imagination rather than real life.

focus (FOH kuhs) *verb* To **focus** is to concentrate on one thing.

G

group (groop) *noun* A **group** is a number of individuals who have things in common, such as family, community, work, or interests.

I

identify (y DEN tuh fy) *verb* When you **identify** something, you recognize or describe it.

ignore (ig NOHR) *verb* To **ignore** something, pay no attention to it.

image (I mij) *noun* An **image** is a mental picture of something.

individual (in duh VIJ wuhl) *noun* An **individual** is one person.

inform (in FAWRM) *verb* When you **inform** people, you communicate information or knowledge to them.

information (in fuhr MAY shuhn) *noun*

If you have **information** about something, you know the facts about it.

inquire (in KWYR) *verb* When you **inquire** about something, you ask questions about it.

insight (IN syt) *noun* When you have **insight** into an idea or a problem, you understand it clearly.

interview (IN tuhr vyoo) *noun* In an **interview,** a person asks another person a series of questions.

investigate (in VES tuh gayt) *verb* When you **investigate** something, you find information about it in order to understand it better.

K

knowledge (NAH lij) *noun* **Knowledge** refers to all of the information and ideas that you have learned.

L

learn (luhrn) *verb* You **learn** when you get new information or knowledge about a subject.

listen (LI suhn) *verb* When you **listen,** you pay attention to what you are hearing.

M

mean (meen) *verb* To **mean** is to show or give a sign of something.

media (MEE dee uh) *noun* The **media**

is all the types of communication that reach many people, such as newspapers, TV, or radio.

method (ME thuhd) *noun* A **method** is a certain way of doing something.

misunderstanding (mi suhn duhr STAN ding) *noun* A **misunderstanding** is an incorrect idea of what someone else said or meant.

O

observe (uhb ZUHRV) *verb* To **observe** something is to watch it carefully.

obstacle (AHB sti kuhl) *noun* An **obstacle** is something that blocks a path or keeps someone from doing something.

opposition (ah puh ZI shuhn) *noun* If you feel **opposition** to something, you resist it or are against it.

organize (AWR guh nyz) *verb* When you **organize** something, you use a system to put it in order.

outcome (OWT kuhm) *noun* An **outcome** is a final result.

P

paraphrase (PER uh frayz) *verb* You **paraphrase** when you reword something spoken or written, usually to make the meaning clear.

pattern (PA tuhrn) *noun* A **pattern** is a habit, or way of behaving that does not change.

perceive (puhr SEEV) *verb* When you **perceive** something, you notice it or understand it.

perception (puhr SEP shuhn) *noun* A **perception** is what you see or understand about things that happen around you.

perform (puhr FAWRM) *verb* To **perform** is to do something or to use a special skill, such as dancing or acting.

perspective (puhr SPEK tiv) *noun* One person's **perspective** is a special point of view in judging things or events.

persuade (puhr SWAYD) *verb* When you **persuade** people, you convince them to do or believe something.

plan (plan) *verb* When you **plan** something, you come up with a method or way to do it.

possible (PAH suh buhl) *adjective* When something is **possible,** it can be done or can happen.

prepare (pri PER) *verb* When you **prepare,** you get ready to use or to do something.

produce (pruh DOOS) *verb* To **produce** something is to make it.

Q

question (KWES chuhn) *verb* When you **question** something, you challenge the truth of it.

R

rarely (RAYR lee) *adverb* Something that **rarely** happens does not happen often.

react (ree AKT) *verb* You **react** when you take action in response to another action.

reaction (ree AK shuhn) *noun* A **reaction** to something is a response to it, or an effect of it.

reality (ree A luh tee) *noun* **Reality** is made up of things that exist in the real world.

recall (ri KAWL) *verb* To **recall** something is to remember it.

reflect (ri FLEKT) *verb* An action will **reflect** a belief when it demonstrates what a person is thinking.

relate (ri LAYT) *verb* When you **relate** information, you tell a story or describe an event.

report (ri PAWRT) *noun* A **report** gives information about a subject.

resolution (re zuh LOO shuhn) *noun* A **resolution** is an ending to a problem or a conflict.

reveal (ri VEEL) *verb* When you **reveal** something, you uncover or show something that was hidden.

S

setting (SE ting) *noun* A **setting** tells where and when action takes place.

source (sawrs) *noun* A **source** is a place where something begins.

speak (speek) *verb* When you **speak,** you use your voice to talk.

strategy (STRA tuh jee) *noun* A **strategy** is a set of plans for doing something well.

struggle (STRUH guhl) *verb* When you **struggle** to do something, you find it hard to do yet keep on trying.

style (styl) *noun* A **style** is a particular way of doing something or expressing yourself.

subject (SUHB jikt) *noun* A **subject** is a topic or focus of discussion.

T

teach (teech) *verb* To **teach** is to explain information or to show how to do something.

team (teem) *noun* A **team** is a group of people who work towards a shared goal.

technology (tek NAHL uh jee) *noun* **Technology** is the use of science to solve real-life problems. It is also devices developed from this use of science.

topic (TAH pik) *noun* A **topic** is a subject or general idea.

tradition (truh DI shuhn) *noun* A meaningful belief or habit passed down over time is a **tradition.**

translate (trans LAYT) *verb* When you **translate** something, you say it in another language or another way.

transmit (trans MIT) *verb* To **transmit** a message is to send it, often through a wire or radio waves.

truth (trooth) *noun* **Truth** is something that is correct and supported by facts.

U

understand (uhn duhr STAND) *verb* To **understand** is to know the meaning of something.

understanding (uhn duhr STAN ding) *noun* An **understanding** is a knowledge of what something means.

unify (YOO nuh fy) *verb* To **unify** people is to bring them together.

unique (yoo NEEK) *verb* If something is **unique,** it is one of a kind.

V

various (VER ee uhs) *adjective* When you have **various** things or ideas, you have different kinds.

view (vyoo) *noun* Your **view** of something is your opinion of it.

voice (voys) *verb* When people **voice** their opinions, they speak their mind.

INDEX

Use the index to find out more about real-life topics.

A

allowance, 128–130
  working for, 130–131
Angel Network, 153–154
animals, therapy, 4–7
  caring for, 6
  dogs, 6
  dolphins, 6–7
  horses, 5
arachnophobia, 104–107
athletes. *See also specific athletes*
  age of, 140, 142–143
  as role models, 40–43
attitude, 149–151
Autrey, Wesley, 122

B

Barkley, Charles, 42–43
Bart Simpson, 197, 198
baseball, 42–43
  superstitions in, 19
basketball, 33–35, 41, 181–182
  superstitions in, 19
Beah, Ishmael, 29–31
Bertier, Gerry, 94–95
Boggs, Wade, 19
Boone, Herman, 93–94
Brothers, Joyce, 137–138
Bugs Bunny, 197, 198
bullying, 20–23
  cyber, 161–163
  emotional reactions to, 162
  reasons for, 22, 162
  what to do about, 22–23, 163

C

Cameron, Deborah, 82–83
celebrity, 137–139
  gossip, 138
  role models, 139
  worship syndrome, 138–139
cell phones, 116–119
  in school, 117–119
  text messaging on, 117–118
censorship, 9–11
CEO. *See* chief executive officer
charity, 153–155
  corporate, 154–155
  reasons for, 155
chief executive officer (CEO), 125–126
China
  censorship in, 9–11
  cloud seeding in, 174
chores, 130–131
cloud seeding, 173–175
Columbia, 97
Columbus, Christopher, 84
community service, 192–195
coyotes, 44–47
  in cities, 45–47
  diet, 46
  protecting pets from, 47

D

democracy, 10
Deng, Luol, 32–35
dogs, 6
dolphins, 5–7

E

dreams, 88–91
  meaning of, 90–91
  as "picture thinking," 89
dress code, 169–171. *See also* uniforms
debate, 169–171

E

Edwards, Tryon, 19
empowerment, 150, 179, 183
endangered species, 64, 66–67

F

Favre, Brett, 143
fear, 104–107. *See also* phobia
fingers, crossing, 18
fires, 122–123, 185, 186
fishing, 100–103

G

gardens, 177–179
Garfield, Patricia, 89
global warming, 172
The Golden Shield Project, 10
Google, 9
gossip
  celebrity, 138
  online, 160–163
graffiti, 12–15
  cleanup, 14
  in New York City, 13–14
  reasons for, 15

greeting cards, 113–115
  beginnings of, 113–114
  e-cards, 114–115
  funny, 114
  New Year's, 114
  Valentines, 113
Griffin, Michael, 99

H

happiness, 152–155
Haring, Keith, 14
Hernandez, Jeremy,
  121–122
heroes, 120–123
Hingis, Martina, 61–62
hip-hop, 134–135
Hollander, 139
horses, 5
Hurricane Katrina, 174, 185,
  186–187

I

Internet
  censorship, 9–11
  dangers, 163
  gossip, 161–163
intervention, 156–159
  failed, 159
  reasons for, 157–159

J

"Jack Sparrow," 198
Jenkins, Jennica, 193–194
jobs, dangerous, 100–103
Jonas, Jay, 182, 183

K

Keller, Helen, 150
kinship care, 56–59
Krausman, Paul, 46
Krzyzewski, Mike,
  181–182, 183

L

leadership, 181–183
Ling, Lisa, 182–183
loggers, 102
Lombardi, Vince, 53

M

Marks, Gretchen, 129
Mars, 76–79
  distance to, 77–78
  food/water on, 78–79
McManus, Danny, 142
military
  child-care services, 51
  parents in, 48–51
  women in, 48
money, 125–127, 129–131.
  See also allowance
  management, 130
Morris, Jim, 141–142
music, 132–135
  to express feelings, 134
  types of, 134
Mutombo, Dikembe, 41–43

N

NASA. *See* National
  Aeronautics and Space
  Administration
National Aeronautics and
  Space Administration
  (NASA), 78, 98-99
National Women's Law
  Center, 51
National Youth Rights
  Association (NYRA), 69–70
Native Americans, 84–87
  sacred ground, 86–87
  sports teams named after,
  85–86
Nelson, Martha, 138

P

Pappas, Mikhail, 178
Paxson, John, 35
peace camps, 24–27
Peale, Norman Vincent, 150
phobia, 105–107
  fighting, 106–107
  spider, 104–107
Pierce, Mary, 53–54
Pirates of the Caribbean, 198
positive thinking, 151
*The Power of Positive
  Thinking* (Peale), 150
Prang, Louis, 114

R

RAK. *See* Random Acts of
  Kindness Foundation
Random Acts of Kindness
  Foundation (RAK), 154
rapid-eye movement (REM),
  88
reading to dogs, 6
refugees, 28, 32
  in Sudan, 34
REM. *See* rapid-eye
  movement
Remember the Titans, 93–95
retirement, 69, 70–71
  forced, 71
Ripken, Cal, Jr., 55
ripple effect, 193–195
Roadrunner, 197–198
role models
  athletes as, 40–43
  celebrity, 139
Roosevelt, Franklin D., 106
Rossio, Terry, 198
Rosten, Leo, 191

S

San Diego Wild Animal Park, 65
Scared Straight, 156
Schwarzenegger, Arnold, 187
secrets, 156
self-destructive behavior, 157
  warning signs, 158–159
self-help books, 151
September 11, 2001, 182
Sierra Leone, 29
Smith, Sean, 138
soldiers, child, 28–31
  amount of, 30
  emotional harm suffered by, 30
  rehabilitation for, 31
Sosa, Sammy, 42
space program
  cost of, 96
  inventions from, 98–99
space station, cost of, 98
speaking
  boys v. girls, 80–83
  topics of, 81–82
spiders, fear of, 104–107
sports, 140–143. *See also* athletes
  baseball, 19, 42
  basketball, 19, 33–35, 41, 181–182
  benefits of, 54
  mascots, 85–86
  medicine, 142
  superstitions in, 18–19
  tennis, 61–63
  training camp, 94
Spry, Alize, 122–123
Stanley, James, 177

Staple, Jennifer, 194–195
star power, 126
Stomp, 135
success, 148
Sudan, 32, 34
Sullivan brothers, 49–50
superstitions, 16–19
  in baseball, 19
  in basketball, 19
  beginnings of, 17–18

T

tagging. *See* graffiti
Taki 183, 13, 15
Tannen, Deborah, 82
TASK. *See* Teens Against Senseless Violence
teamwork, 92
Teens Against Senseless Violence (TASK), 177–178
Teens for Humanity (TFH), 194
tennis, 61–63
TFH. *See* Teens for Humanity
tornadoes, 184, 185–186
"The Tortoise and the Hare," 198
traffic accidents, 102
trash collection, 100
tricksters, 196–199
  appeal of, 199
  punishment of, 199

U

Udall, Mark, 175
UNHCR. *See* United Nations High Commissioner for Refugees

uniforms, 169–171
  debate, 169–171
  school pride and, 170
United Nations High Commission for Refugees (UNHCR), 30–31
urban myths, 188–191
  cautionary, 189–190
  food contamination, 190
  frightening, 190
  funny, 190–191
  reasons for repeating, 191
  shock value, 190
  spread of, 188
  sympathy scam, 190

V

voting age, 68–70

W

Washington, Denzel, 93
weather
  disasters, 173, 184–187
  modification, 172–175
Wile E. Coyote, 197–198
Williams, Jason, 181
Williams, Serena, 61–63
Williams, Venus, 61–63
Winfrey, Oprah, 125, 153–154
  Angel Network, 153–154
Woods, Tiger, 125, 126
World Sports Humanitarian Hall of Fame, 43

Z

zoos, 65–67
  breeding programs in, 66
  disagreement over, 66–67

CREDITS

Illustrations
Marcelo Baez 2-3, 38-39, 74-75, 110-111, 146-147, 166-167.

Maps
XNR Productions, Inc.: 25, 34.

Photographs
Every effort has been made to secure permission and provide appropriate credit for photographic material. The publisher deeply regrets any omission and pledges to correct errors called to its attention in subsequent editions.

Unless otherwise acknowledged, all photographs are the property of Pearson Education.

Photo locators denoted as follows:
Top (T), Center (C), Bottom (B), Left (L), Right (R), Background (Bkgd)

Cover (Bkgd L) Dorling Kindersley/DK Images, (Bkgd C) Mike Peters, (Bkgd R) Jay Blakesberg/Jupiter Images, (L) Getty Images, (C) Tom Grill/Corbis (CR) Jamie Marshall/DK Images; (BR) Chase Jarvis/Digital Vision/Getty Images; 5 Judi Ashlock/iStockphoto; 6 Frank Greenaway/Dorling Kindersley; 9 iStockphoto; 13 Jan Matoška/Shutterstock; 17 Chiya Lee/iStockphoto; 21 Izabela Habur/iStockphoto; 26 Alberto Pomares/iStockphoto; 29, Patrick Robert/Sygma/Corbis; 30, WireImage/Getty Images; 33, NBAE/Getty Images; 41 Gary Dineen/Getty Images; 45 Yanik Chauvin/Shutterstock; 49 U.S. Naval Historical Center/Naval Historical Center; 53 Big Stock Photo; 54 Phil Anthony/Shutterstock; 57 Karen Struthers/Shutterstock; 61 Reuters/Corbis; 65 Mila Hutchinson/iStockphoto; 66 Kitch Bain/iStockphoto; 69 David Frazier/PhotoEdit; 77 NASA; 81 Chris Schmidt/iStockphoto; 85 Jose Gil/Shutterstock; 86 Silver-John/Shutterstock; 89 Franzelin Franz-W./Shutterstock; 93 Getty Images; 97 NASA; 101 Christopher Pillitz/Getty Images; 105 Judex/Shutterstock; 106 Cathy Keifer/iStockphoto; 113 Christina Kennedy/fStop/Getty Images; 114 Marek Slusarczyk/iStockphoto; 117 Rob Marmion/Shutterstock; 121 Lawrence Sawyer/iStockphoto; 122 Scott Schnelder/Getty Images; 125 Andy Altenburger/Icon SMI/Corbis; 126 Melissa Madia/iStockphoto; 129 Bonnie Jacobs/iStockphoto; 133 Library of Congress; 134 Anatema/Shutterstock; 137 Pavel Losevsky/iStockphoto; 138 iStockphoto; 141 AP Images; 149 (L) Chris Schmidt/iStockphoto, (R) Joseph C. Justice Jr./iStockphoto; 153 HFHI/Steffan Hacker/Habitat for Humanity International; 154 Jeff Greenberg/PhotoEdit; 157 Robert Churchill/iStockphoto; 158 Christina Kennedy/Getty Images; 161 Justin Horrocks/iStockphoto; 169 Valueline/Punchstock; 173 Chan Pak Kei/iStockphoto; 177 CNCS Photo Office; 178 CNCS Photo Office; 181 Kevin C. Cox/Getty Images; 185 Robert A. Mansker/Shutterstock; 186 Wendy Kaveney Photography/Shutterstock; 189 Randall Stevens/Shutterstock; 190 Kristen Johansen/iStockphoto;193 Andreea Angelescu/Corbis; 194 David H. Lewis/iStockphoto; 197 Douglas Kirkland/Corbis.